MY PRIVATE CHINA

Alex Kuo

BLACKSMITH BOOKS

My Private China

ISBN 978-988-16139-4-3

Published by Blacksmith Books
5th Floor, 24 Hollywood Road, Hong Kong
Tel: (+852) 2877 7899
www.blacksmithbooks.com

Cover design by Catherine Tai

"In *My Private China* Alex Kuo plays with the multiple realities of Tiananmen Square China, global China, and post-colonial China. The shifting scales of ancient, present and future merge into a meditation on China's place and China's space. Though he may reveal that the tank gun barrels in 1989 Tiananmen were plugged, Kuo is certainly unplugged in this insightful collection."
– R. Edward Grumbine, author of *Where the Dragon Meets the Angry River*

"With irony, wit and intelligence, Alex Kuo shares his unique experiences in China and Hong Kong. Part memoir, part cultural analysis, *My Private China* skewers stereotypes and misconceptions with the sharp eye and beautiful prose of the novelist and poet he is also. This is a must-read for China watchers and anyone willing to get behind the lazy reporting and political posturing that so often informs writing about China." – Robert Abel, author of *Riding a Tiger*

This book is for Joan, who continues to lead me into trouble.

Also by Alex Kuo:

The Window Tree
New Letters from Hiroshima and Other Poems
Changing the River
Chinese Opera
Lipstick and Other Stories
This Fierce Geography
Panda Diaries
White Jade and Other Stories
A Chinaman's Chance
The Man Who Dammed the Yangtze

Acknowledgement to the following publications in which earlier versions of all but two of these essays first appeared, some under different titles: *Biblio, The Bloomsbury Review, The Bridge Bulletin, Calapooya, Greenfield Review, Hong Kong-iMail, Idahonian, Journal of Ethnic Studies, Lipstick and Other Stories, Many Mountains Moving, Mascara, Piano Journal, Ploughshares, Seattle Post-Intelligencer, Seattle Times, Universe, The World Today.*

CONTENTS

INTRODUCTION

Two years after I was born at Boston's MGH just months before Hermann Göring's Junkers and Stukas bombed "defenceless-under-the-night" Poland to begin World War II, my mother took me back to her hometown of Suzhou on Shanghai's western sprawl. On the day the war ended when Paul Tibbets' *Enola Gay* dropped the world's first weapon of mass destruction on Hiroshima, I was old and awake enough to see the flash of its holocaust several hundred miles away at seven on a sweltering Shanghai summer morning.

The family left for Hong Kong two years before the venerable Chairman Mao proclaimed China's liberation atop Beijing's Gate of Heavenly Peace (Tiananmen Square) on October 1, 1949. After attending a Canadian order of the Immaculate Conception Tak Sun elementary school and then the British high school for mainly children of expatriates, King George V near the old Kai Tak airport from where we could see RAF de Havilland Vampire fighters on practice runs, I returned to the United States for college and graduate work.

Beginning with a fall semester of teaching American literature at Beijing Forestry University following the political spring at Tiananmen Square in 1989, in the last twenty-five years

I have returned to and left China and Hong Kong almost every other year, sometimes staying a year at a time. Sometimes as a Senior Fulbright or Lingnan Scholar, sometimes on a United Nations or Idaho Commission for the Arts research grant, and sometimes on my own dime, I taught American studies and translation to undergraduates, graduates and faculties at universities such as Peking, Beijing Foreign Studies and Tsinghua in Beijing, Chengdu Science and Technology, Hong Kong and Hong Kong Baptist, Jilin University in Changchun, and Shanghai's Fudan, which appointed me its first Distinguished Writer-in-Residence in 2008, a first for any Chinese university.

Numerous short stories, novels and poems were written during this period about China and Hong Kong, and of course, the profiles, essays and interviews in this collection. All but two of them have been previously published in magazines and newspapers in the U.S., U.K., Australia and Hong Kong.

Through an exploration of living in China and Hong Kong, they were written and sent home to help me and my friends make sense of what I was experiencing, and how this personal sense of place shapes our political consciousness and understanding of the other—why people get up in the morning, what they do during the day, and what's their last thought before falling asleep, their dreams, wishes and lies.

They can also be read as transPacific public essays (sometimes in narrative form, sometimes in conversation with essential informants such as novelist and Cultural Minister (1986-89) Wang Meng, Chairman Mao's confidant Professor Li, and the winner of the Schumann Competition, pianist Madame Zhou Guangren, teacher of Lang Lang), that look from the outside in and inside out, from the altitude of a Boeing 747 at 30,000 feet, a distance of five thousand miles away at a Seattle Starbucks, or just a few minutes north of Beijing at the Great Wall at Badaling. They look at China more than just as a place, something more important than the practical information about its weather, places to stay, or currency. Hopefully this look at the other China will place us in a better position to understand its current economic explosion and what that will mean for the lives of its peoples in their Century of the Dragon.

Section 1

Tiananmen Square, 1989 and Later

TANKS ON TIANANMEN SQUARE

Ge sorted through his files in the newspaper office and pulled out the photographs he had saved in the last nineteen years for his front-page lead on Tiananmen Square. First, the AP photo taken of someone identified as Wang Weilin a.k.a. Tank Man on June 5, 1989 by Jeff Widener hiding half a mile away with a 400 mm lens in a sixth-floor room of the Beijing Hotel. Or one by *Life*'s Stuart Franklin that won him a World Press Award taken maybe two rooms away on the same floor of the same hotel where foreign correspondents clustered at the rooftop bar at five every afternoon to verify each other's stories. Or another by *Newsweek*'s Charlie Cole, same date, same time, same subject.

Ge flipped to a page in his worn copy of a 1999 issue of *Time* magazine in which Tank Man had morphed into Unknown Rebel and was designated one of the 100 Most Influential Persons of the entire 20th century. With a book bag in one hand and a flag in the other waving a column of People's Liberation Army Norinco Type 59 main battle tanks into submission at Tiananmen[2], he was designated a global human rights hero. We don't need a flag here, not now. Testifying at a House International Relations Human Rights subcommittee meeting in Washington seven years later, Amnesty International's Louisa Coan identified him as a student. Right. Now we have a flag to wave. We have public memory.

He looked at these tank photos again. Their gun barrels were plugged—no tank drivers were going to be given the option of opening up their 100 mm cannons in T^2 regardless of I.Q., training or experience. No battalion commander was going to take the chance that an errant shell might damage Chairman Mao's Mausoleum or Gate of Heavenly Peace. Just bring in the tanks for intimidation and crowd control. To show who's the boss, who's in charge here.

Now, who was that man in front of the tanks who refused to be intimidated and what happened to him? Ge opened another file. A former special assistant to President Nixon reported ten years later that the masked man was executed fourteen days afterwards. Another file claimed he was shot months later. Still others held out, hopeful he had somehow escaped to Taiwan, in 1949 or forty years later in 1989, or was just laying low in Chengdu until the right movie script came along.

Just maybe he was an intelligence agent marking out the picket line for the tank drivers, and the book bag held his field radio to HQ? Maybe he was a bored Bank of China accountant who had too much to drink for lunch. Maybe he was just caught up in the moment and, aware that the lights were on and cameras rolling worldwide, acted out the expected role before Steven Spielberg or Mel Gibson or David Wolper had a chance.

Ge could not write any of this in American free-style and not sound Chinese, however appropriate the anger and the fury; and he could not write this in Chinese because no American would ever believe him. But maybe none of this mattered, since he was not writing fiction, remember? He was doing journalism. So Ge thought as he looked at the last picture again, the end. The best part was over, he'd missed it, he had come in too late. But that's all he's got, this one picture. This was the only memory that has been recorded, all the emotions coalesced into this one visual icon, and nothing is going to change any of it, nothing. It has become history, in the same way as *Gone with the Wind,* the memory moving forward and backward in the absolute present.

(When I was at Shanghai's Fudan University in 2008, I met the cultural critic for the *North China Daily News*. He had a Ph.D. in ethics, which he said made him the biggest loser in all of Shanghai. He wanted to write a book about the influence of film and visual icons on public memory, which he doubted anyone in Shanghai or anywhere else would be interested in. I also learned about his fixation on the 1939 film *Gone with the Wind*, especially its distortions of racial relations in the United States at the time of the Civil War. To one of these dinners, he had brought along a worn copy of the ten-year-old *Time* magazine that featured Tiananmen Square's Tank Man as one of the 100 most influential persons of the 20th century. Over several beers, he was exceptionally articulate about his disdain for the media's duplicity in the construction of such a political consciousness, especially when it's based on a photograph of ambiguous and ubiquitous meaning. I have transferred his personal narrative almost *verbatim* to this fictional protagonist Ge, extracted from my novel-in-progress *shanghai.shanghai.shanghai.*)

BOOKS AND POLITICS

My interpreter Shi Baohui and I arrived early at the main gate of the Ministry of Culture's offices in downtown Beijing, where the security was still visibly prominent after the June 4 government crackdown on the student demonstrations.

A soldier with a holstered sidearm checked the identification of everyone going in and out of the walled compound, while another watched from a small shelter, clipboard in hand, sitting at a table with a telephone and tea service for two. He verified the work IDs with photo insets, or sealed and stamped invitations, while his partner made the occasional telephone call for further authentication.

Since we did not have the appropriate credentials, we stood and waited: the telephone call agreeing to this interview that came from Wang Meng's secretary Saturday, instructed me to wait for him at the main gate.

Shi was in his mid 30s. With a British graduate education in linguistics, he was dressed in suit and sweater, like most Chinese professors of both genders in Beijing's numerous language and literature centers (spelled *centre*), institutes and universities.

He was beginning to act nervous on this warm, sunny and beautiful afternoon exactly one week after the capital had quietly celebrated the 40th birthday of his modernizing nation. The leaves of the many maple, locust and ginkgo trees lining the broad downtown avenues were just beginning to change color. There were still many blossoms left on plants, particularly red and yellow chrysanthemums, partly from the previous week's National Day celebrations. There were also many wasps out.

I tried to distract Shi by talking to him about those yellow jackets, *hymenoptera-vespidae*, how at this time of the year at my home in Idaho they were not to be trusted. I also told him about some friends who named their dog after the famous sumo wrestler Taiho and who liked to snap at them, but Shi was not paying any attention. He was looking for an official to meet us, and he was late.

A young man in a windbreaker came out to the gate and began chatting with one of the soldiers. Shi and he eyed each other for several minutes before Shi walked over and introduced himself, and then they both said something else and laughed. I understood enough to know that the young man, presumably one of Wang Meng's secretaries, was looking for an American, meaning a white person.

I walked over and there were more introductions, some in Chinese, some in English. At the gate, the soldier formally bowed to me, but I was distracted from its meaning by an awkward but familiar moment.

"After you."

"No, you, you first."

"No, you are V.I.P."

At last inside the gate, we turned to the right of the courtyard. Several women with wet hair came out of a side building. They were drying and combing their hair and having a good time in the fall sunshine, laughing, joking. It appeared to be customary for large institutions such as government agencies and joint-venture hotels to provide their lower-level (i.e. lower-salaried) personnel with showering facilities at their place of work, and with places to nap during the customary *wu xu* between 12:00 and 2:00 every work day because most of them had no hot water, tubs or showers where they lived.

Away from the laughter of the women around the next left was a small parking lot filled with fancy cars, stretch, black Mercedes with all-around tinted glass, their uniformed drivers hand-buffing the polish. Some of these cars had black, diplomatic license plates. Unlike the atmosphere of the previous block, the male drivers were quiet, intent on their work. A 1968 black Ford Mustang GT 390 in mint condition parked alone in a shaded corner surprised me.

They were busy, tall gray office buildings constructed most in the last 30 years and resembling eastern Europe's no-frills architectural response to a burgeoning, centralized bureaucracy, everywhere inside this compound whose walls were topped with shards of glass and barb wired. Around another right after the parking lot, the three of us faced another walled, simulated, older native-styled formal courtyard with one single-storied traditional building inside. There were no visible phone or power lines inside this compound.

Shi and I were passed off to a man waiting at the gate to the inner courtyard. In suit and tie in his early 40s, he didn't look like a bureaucrat, but more like a Public Security Bureau agent whom I had seen managing security at the Great Hall of the People state dinner two weeks ago, who looked more like the captain of a Yale crew come back for a class reunion.

But at this moment he was very serious, an interpreter for the Minister of Culture looking me over, making sure that I was who I was, *The Journal of Ethnic Studies'* literary editor, Washington State University faculty member, and American writer, as he knew me. I could not engage his eyes in a non-official look. (Later he was to scribble notes on his white pad throughout the interview, and from ten feet away, his sharp eyes did not miss the opportunity to correct several misspelled names in my notes.)

After the introductions at the gate, he said "After you" in English with a British accent.

"No, you first."

"You are the V.I.P."

The side courtyard was spacious, a formal garden landscaped from trees, flowers, and carefully spaced stone steps, the office building atmosphere of its immediate outside completely masked. We walked into the main entrance of the small building that didn't look as if it was any larger than the conference room we had stepped into. This was also spacious, with orderly, traditional landscape paintings on scrolls on the walls, subdued lighting and not a table in sight. The numerous soft chairs were strategically arranged to accommodate meetings of any combination of more than two persons.

Li Jian the interpreter invited Shi and me to make ourselves comfortable while he went to "fetch" Wang Meng. We did not know if we should sit, but we did anyway, next to each other at the end of one long row of velvet-covered, deep-green chairs. I got out my notes, my notebook and pen, a gift for Wang, and began to wonder how long we would have to wait for a 30-minute meeting, the time we had agreed to on the phone.

Wang appeared within two minutes. About five feet nine in a dark brown suit with a light blue shirt and dark brown tie with a lighter brown sweater and glasses, it was obvious he had worked through the noon break and had not taken the customary *wu xu*.

"I am very happy to meet you," he said in English.

We sat down. That is, the two interpreters sat down, but Wang and I mimed around to see who should sit first, and I was reminded of a similar episode involving my father and Chiang Kai-shek just before his imminent exile to Taiwan. Finally Wang sat down first, at my insistence. We sat side-by-side on the same sofa, Shi around the bend to Wang's left, and Li in a single chair to my immediate right. We had destroyed the interior decorator's seating plan for four: communications psychologists would have reacted negatively to our seating arrangement. A woman in a janitorial blue blazer brought in four cups of tea. Only Shi touched his.

"Congratulations for leaving your administrative appointment to return to your work. Congratulations," I said to him in English.

"Thank you for understanding. You are first, you are writer," Wang said, also in English.

"I would like to take notes of this meeting. Would you prefer this interview to be private, or would you not mind my publishing some of it?"

"No, no, you can take notes, as many as you want."

"What will you be doing when you leave the Ministry?" I asked, taking it slowly, already knowing the answer.

"I will write a long novel."

"What about?" I laughed and he laughed, both of us knowing the meaning in the question. Our two interpreters looked confused, but also perturbed that at this point it appeared as if their presence was unnecessary.

"It would be about changes in Chinese society since 1949," Wang answered in Chinese, explaining that there have been many. [The year 1949 kept on reappearing in conversations and floral displays around Beijing. On October 1, 1949, Mao Zedong declared China the People's Republic of China, PRC. This was 1989, its 40th anniversary.] Shi started to translate, but I shook him off.

Wang continued in Chinese, and wanted to know about me, more than what he had read in my resume. Shi answered for me in Chinese, Wang nodding. Wang wanted to know specifically what universities my father had been president of, and I wanted to know what specific changes in China he would write his novel about, and if he saw himself as a novelist documenting the individualized histories of a country, but I answered his questions instead.

Wang looked good, a bit tired, but basically good. We continued in English and in Chinese, Wang not hesitating to insert Chinese words and phrases in the middle of an English sentence (a very refreshing change from most conversations I got into in Beijing where they insisted on using only English words, thereby turning the conversation into baby-talk or tourist-walk), most of which I understood, some of which were translated by Li, and some by Shi when Li could not understand all of my English or could not find the English equivalent for Wang's rhetoric.

Wang looked young for his age, and did not look as if he had been recently betrayed. He was warm, open, sincere and calm, that is until the last two questions of the interview. He wore his glasses, except to take them off to squint at the inscription inside the copy of my last book that I gave him. Contrary to the September 18 *Time* magazine's misinforming and irresponsible article that claimed he had been deposed and had not been seen in months, I was convinced that Wang had not been forced to step down from his administrative duties, but that his departure was voluntary, to return to his own work, that the three-year term, the original condition for accepting the appointment, had expired.

For the moment we both forgot China's long tradition of writers also serving their country by being government administrators, Jiang Qing notwithstanding. I avoided the tacky and did not ask him if he had voluntarily stepped away from the Minister of Culture position, if he had been deposed, if he had been sacked, if the resignation scenario was just a public hedge against being criticized; nor did I ask him about the meaning of the recent April-June Tiananmen Square incident.

"Which novel of yours is the most important to you?" I asked instead.

"I think *Movable Parts*, in 1986," he answered after a moment thinking about the question.

"Has it been translated?"

"Yes, into Italian and Russian. I was in Turin when it came out."

I then proceeded to describe in Chinese *The Journal of Ethnic Studies'* plans to commit eight issues of 64-page insert on a different color paper, for a selection of younger, contemporary Chinese writers, and asked if he would help in connecting with these writers.

"Yes, I'll be glad to," he answered in English.

Would he let us inaugurate the series with two of his own short stories?

"Yes, of course."

Would he help me to contact some editors as well?

"Yes. Wang Mingjie is no longer editor of *Chinese Literature,* he has been promoted up to a director's job with the foreign languages presses. *Chinese Literature* is now edited by Yin Shuxin, a Muslim, you know, but not like the Ayatollah Khomeini. Everyone on the staff of *Chinese Literature* knows Chinese, English and French. You can also contact the monthly *Poetry* edited by Chang Zhimin, with a 70,000 circulation."

Who were some young Chinese writers today whose work he admired?

Zhang Cheng Zhi, Wang Anyi, both fiction writers. Wang Anyi was 32, whose mother was also a novelist [though she had not published since 1957, the year that began the mandatory rehabilitation period], both from Shanghai.

"Yes, of course; I will phone them."

[Two days after the interview, I received calls from the editors of *Chinese Literature* and *Poetry,* as well as two stories in the mail from Wang Meng.]

We then discussed readerships. In China, a book of poetry did well if it sold between 1,000 and 2,000 copies. (For an economic comparison, a full professor at the prestigious Peking University made ¥180 a month, slightly more than a street-sweeper's salary, while a piano player who played two hours a day and three days a week at the Yanshan Hotel bar made ¥2,500 a month.)

At this point I gave him a copy of my most recent book, a slim volume of poetry, mentioning that it had sold about 1,000 copies in two years. He took off his glasses to squint at the inscription inside. He liked poetry, he said in Chinese, and read some lines from the book, adding in English, "I will enjoy reading this later."

"Do you have any plans to have your novels published in English?"

"There is a Jennifer [he could not remember her last name] from London. We have corresponded several times. She is an agent and she has a translator [presumably Cathy Silber], and some chapters of *Movable Parts* have been translated."

"How about a U.S. publication?"

"English is English, whether it's England or the United States."

There was high energy in this meeting, but so far the questions and answers had been very polite and quite pedestrian.

"What do you think of the Pioneer School of Fiction," I asked.

Wang looked confused. The interpreters looked confused. My own literal translation with the help of a dictionary of Chinese literary terms had backfired. I mentioned a writer, Bei Dao. I mentioned another one, Liu Xinwu. I mentioned a third one, Yu Luojin. The three of them conferred. These were writers loved by the Hong Kong readers.

There is a very significant similarity between the Hong Kong Chinese and the Miami Cubans: they both live with idealized political constructs, they both claim to love their motherland but hate its current politics and try to influence them from a distance, they both look to the West for myths to teach them how to live and what to believe in, regardless of how many times they have been betrayed, misunderstood and misrepresented by its public, media, Hollywood, missionaries, or by the CIA, FBI, MI6 or the State Department.

"New Wave. Yes. New Wave School," Wang finally said, excited. It was obvious he didn't like them. "They don't write about politics. They don't write about society's problems. They have no characters. They have no heroes. They have no meaning. The writers have a complete free hand. They break all the traditions of literature. They do not have the opportunity to experience Western life and they do not have the opportunity to read Western literature; but they think they are like the Western writers from film, and live and write in this modern way in the imagination. In the imagination. It is not true; what they write is not true."

"What do you think is the role of literature in a socialist, modernizing nation?"

He didn't like this question. His voice changed, and then in Chinese he quibbled about which socialist nation. But he knew what I meant and said that the reading of literature will improve the literacy of the nation. He added that literature will give the people something to do in the evening.

"In many countries literature had been closely associated with politics. Why do you think that in the United States, literature is not commonly regarded as important by the public? And in fact many of the literature professors there don't even read what has been written in the last century," I asked.

His answer, this time in Chinese, was better. First he said that in London two years ago he met many writers who were concerned with political issues, mentioning meeting Margaret Drabble and Salman Rushdie before the notoriety of *The Satanic Verses*. Then he said that in these countries the readers' attention was distracted by too many social activities, that people in these countries didn't feel politics everyday, like in China, where politics is experienced from morning to night everyday, where one could not close their eyes to the political realities around them. "You have to understand this," he emphasized in English.

He didn't provide the linking argument, and I looked to his interpreter, Li, who had kept the same expression all along, even through the jokes. Shi's eyes told me I had asked too much.

We then talked about Margaret Thatcher and Ronald Reagan's oppressive influence on education and literature and the arts, and about Reagan's unsuccessful attempt to give his papers to Stanford University, but we both knew the interview was over with the last two questions.

Wang looked at his watch. It was 4:30, one hour past the designated time for the interview. Everyone got up at once.

On the way out he spoke in Chinese in an aside to Shi in a very friendly tone of voice. On the bicycle ride back, I did not ask Shi what Wang had said to him, but wondered if Wang Meng will be the first Chinese writer to receive the Nobel Award for literature soon.

(Born in Beijing on October 15, 1934, Wang Meng was raised in Hebei Province, but moved back to the safety of Beijing after the July 7th Incident in 1937.

Wanting to be a professional revolutionary, Wang joined the Chinese Communist Party in 1948, five days before turning fourteen, and for the next nine years he became politically active in the Beijing Youth League. In 1952, after failing the university entrance examinations for a course of study in architectural engineering so that he could participate "on the front line of national construction," he decided to become a writer, having been influenced by the Russian novelist S.P. Antonov's *Number One Profession.*

While waiting for the editorial response to his first finished work, the novel *Long Live Youth!*, his short story "Little Dou-er" was published in *People's Literature*, one-third censored and its title changed. Encouraged by the Chinese Writers Association and the Youth Publishing House, Wang nevertheless started revising his novel *Long Live Youth!* In typeset and the final galley stage, it was prevented from publication in the 1957 Anti-Rightist Campaign, and did not appear in print until 1979, more than 20 years later.

Expelled from the party, between 1958 and 1962 Wang performed manual labor on the outskirts of Beijing; and from 1963 to 1979, he "remolded" and "reformed" his thinking in the northwestern Xinjiang Province, where he "lived and toiled" with the Uygur minority peasants. Protected by them and the local cadres, he did not suffer any personal abuse during the ten chaotic years of the Cultural Revolution between 1966 and 1976, "nothing short of a miracle."

After the fall of the Gang of Four and his subsequent reinstatement as a party member, in the summer of 1979 Wang moved back with his family to Beijing, where he continued to write. Since then his major publications include *Long Live Youth!* (also made into a movie which every middleschooler in China has seen), *Winter Rain, Selected Fiction, Deep Lake, The Strain of Meeting, Selected Novellas, The Jacket at the Bottom of the Trunk, Light Gray Eyes, The Movable Parts, The Famous Doctor Liang Youzhi*, as well as collections of travel essays, literary criticism, and translations from the Uygur.

In June of 1980 Wang visited West Germany before spending the fall at the University of Iowa's International Writers' Program, where he wrote the novella *Dapple* in the Mayflower Apartments in Iowa City. In the spring of 1986, Wang had his first foreign publication, the short story "Kite Streamers," in *The Journal of Ethnic Studies, 14:1*, and participated as a special guest and delegation head in the 48th meeting of International P.E.N. Association held in New York.

In September of 1985, Wang was elected to the Chinese Communist Party's inner Party Central Committee, and in May of 1986, he assumed the duties of China's Minister of Culture. I interviewed him at his official office just after Beijing's political spring of 1989, and just before he was asked to step down from this significant cultural and political position.

His generosity at introducing me to several contemporary young poets resulted in my translation class working on them initially before Sherman Alexie later completed the translations and final editing. In 1991 they became his first professional publications.

I also learned much later that Wang Meng's work had generated some serious repercussions in China as well as abroad when it satirized China's helmsman Deng Xiaoping, raising questions about when his writing was serious and when he was joking. A line from one of his short stories published in December 1998 which said that "our countrymen are fond of unity" was taken literally by inept foreign readers as well as Beijing's censors, when clearly his intention was sarcasm.)

COUNTING

As often as Li told Mao to be careful, the head librarian would always find out, if not today, then tomorrow, or the day after, and without warning, she would emerge from behind a stack or cart and the two of them would have to answer her same question repeated again and again. "Why are you here, to work or read?" "If you just want to read, go home and read." "Think, think, why are you here?" No answer was acceptable— she was the head librarian.

After the two of them were caught in the modern history section for the third time in as many days, both Li and Mao were sacked from their library jobs, thus ending their formal education at Beida. "You must remember we were very young then," Professor Li reminded me almost exactly seventy years later, "over there, there," pointing his walking cane towards the city below us without looking.

So out of the students' dormitory, the two of them carried all their belongings, bedrolls on their backs, some clothes, their *fanhes*, but mostly books secreted out of the library in their imaginations, and went into the Beijing streets that early May, 1919, looking for a place to stay. Some friends took them in, after they promised not to hold any secret meetings, a rigidly enforced covenant that was beginning to see some disappearances.

Li knew it was doubtful the two of them would stay there long, but they were determined, not wanting to involve their friends in something irreversible. In fact, after the first two days, Li and Mao never returned, leaving everything, everything except their chance.

Our teacups were shaking on the table. At first I thought Professor Li had hit a leg of the table with his cane again.

"Tremors, just tremors," he said. "It happens here a lot."

But in 1900 there was more, but more was not enough, so it shook again in 1911, 1919, 1928 and 1966. Now his granddaughter cared by his side, though he could well do it himself, his count still reliable. A doctor of the heart, she had requested a work unit transfer here to be close to her grandfather. What she counted was entirely different, if she counted at all past the pulse, that she allowed me to see in her eyes just once on the second day of the interview.

After 1919, Li and Mao separated, occasionally reappearing together in the most unusual of places. When Mao took his arduous hike to Shaanxi Province in the winter of 1935, Li welcomed him at Yan'an and invited him to his son's wedding. On a flight over the Hump in 1944, a Flying Tiger pilot must have seen the two of them huddled together in the cargo hold, planning strategy amidst the filing cabinets and Steinway CD he was hauling around China for Madame Chiang just one gas tank ahead of her imminent defection to Taiwan.

"What was he like? What was old *huxi dai you suan wei* like, standing there on that autumn afternoon at the Gate of Heavenly Peace?"

His close friends and trusted theoreticians called him *garlic breath,* his doctors advised him to quit smoking, and one warm night that summer, he personally rode around the capital putting his initials on every one of its forty-nine trolleys and five buses. But on October 1, 1949, nothing else seemed to matter. He was already a monument there atop the review stands at the Gate of Heavenly Peace, facing south in the tumultuous afternoon sunlight, the city thronging with a million red and yellow chrysanthemums. Professor Li and his son were with him, standing to his right, sharing his limelight, but they all knew the work had just begun.

"I was born the next year," Professor Li's granddaughter added, her only words within my hearing that weekend.

"Yes," Professor Li added, "yes, and she would have been baptized by the bishop at Nantang if the Vatican had not ordered the Chinese Catholics to stop reading Chinese newspapers and wearing red scarves, wearing red scarves, red scarves, as in 1966, under red banners, there suddenly appeared at Beida's south gate, teenagers all, storming the gatekeepers, chanting, grabbing the head librarian by her hair and beating her to death, along with her father, my only son."

Yes, his granddaughter was in the middle of high school that year, and some of her classmates were responsible. Nevertheless she blamed Mao for doing nothing, Professor Li said, and looked away.

"And in two years she went away to medical school, what there was left of any healing."

There were no benches. "Count them," he said, "there were no benches, not one, not a single one."

The three of us sat there counting, one empty space after another in the yellowing photograph of that October afternoon.

It must have reminded her of the night her father died, I imagined, as she bent down to kiss him this one last time with no smell of tobacco on his breath, on the night he died, baby, come hug, come hug and say goodbye, come baby, come hug.

Sometimes our nerves are like that, brought about by our own carelessness, ignoring storm warnings, plain forgetting, or just looking the other way for no reason at all.

"What did you think, what did you think though as you stood there next to him with your son who would soon father a daughter and then be beaten to death by her classmates before she finished high school?"

"There were no benches in sight, that is to say, there were no benches. Everyone was standing up, shouting, waving tiny red flags. It's true, RKO News was there, recording it all. Edward Murrow too, but I don't think he saw any benches either. Even if he had seen any, he would not have mentioned it in his broadcasts, since nobody in America would have cared."

"So why were you counting benches when you knew there weren't any on the review stands or in the square that you could not see anyway?"

In the past perfect tense of Chinese grammar, he suggested that while he stood there between Old Garlic Breath and his son, he had anticipated this inevitable calamity. That is the price. There is no other way to translate this.

What eventually brought us back could have been anything, the granddaughter getting up to replenish our tea, a tree in the courtyard shimmering in the light, anything at all. Who was there to say why the breathing stopped, if it had stopped at all? Why were our voices filled with double meanings?

"You know," Professor Li added, "he was always afraid of the cold."

Yes, we know, yes, though sometimes not by name, yes. Baby, come, come say hug, come say goodbye. The heart is such an extravagant organ.

(On October 1, 1949, when photographers were busily taking historical pictures of Mao Zedong proclaiming the establishment of the People's Republic of China atop the review stands in Beijing's Tiananmen Square, Professor Li Weibin, Mao's confidant and trusted advisor, was standing by his side. You can see him in his long coat and glasses in the photographs that were shot from the west.

Last month [1989] I interviewed him in his home in the Fragrant Hills outside Beijing, the same location that prompted much of Cao Xueqin's *Dream of the Red Chamber*. More than ninety years old by most accounts, Professor Li was collected, lucid, and did not make a single error of time, place or identity.

The visit extended over the entire weekend, and as he and his granddaughter bade their farewells at the gates on Sunday evening, he confided to me his wish to see his story published as soon as possible.)

DEFINITIONS

Shun Min was assigned the news anchoring position right after graduation from the national broadcasting institute. At three hours a day, ten days a month, no writing or editing or reporting stories, just show up in time for makeup before noon and before six to read the news, it was easy enough, the envy of his classmates who were given jobs as video librarian, station timekeeper and boom operators.

For the first two years he put all of himself into his work, each story he read, however short and sometimes ambiguous, carried his most sincere and believable expressions, his voice pulsing with heart-felt humanity, assuring his viewers of the safe passage of another day. *Trust me, trust me* he said at least five hundred times a year in the privacy of four million Beijing homes, *I will not lie to you*, and the people in the capital believed him, even when the lights sometimes reflected off his glasses. On the streets he was easy to recognize, and pedestrians would stop him and express their trust, sometimes touching a hand or sleeve, and once, in this country where things numinous have been banned since its liberation in 1949, an elderly woman limping on her left side lightly tugged one of his ears just to make sure he was not divinity itself.

This April when he was reading a brief story on the evening news about the student gathering at Tiananmen Square, a wisp of anxiety appeared in his eyes, and for the remaining minutes before the camera shifted to the international weather map, his voice sounded distracted, then stumbled once on the temperature between Karachi and Cairo.

After the broadcast, the news producer approached him, concerned about his health and diet. The station manager offered a car to take him home. Slightly cautious from all this attention, he said *I'm all right* carefully three times before they believed him, then rode his bicycle home after wiping off his makeup going down in the elevator. In the approaching twilight of another promising spring sunset, Shun wondered about riding downtown to see the students, but not being a reporter, he went home instead, mentally counting the number of times these students have gathered here in Beijing: 1900, 1911. 1927. 1966, 1976, and now in 1989, seven times this century although he was not sure 1966 should be included.

That evening as he continued reading another reformist novelist preoccupied with the scar on the national conscience left there by the three years of political aberration between 1966 and 1969—a wound so deep even now a generation later people still refuse to talk about it, as if it had completely vanished, or had not happened at all, which Shun knew was not true—he heard a loud knocking on his apartment door. All evening he had heard the repeated sirens of police and emergency vehicles passing in the streets, and the excited but low voices of his neighbors who had gone to investigate the rumors, but as a news professional, he knew that such compulsive curiosity could wait until the stories came into the studio in the morning, after they had been gathered, sorted and vetted by knowledgeable persons trained and experienced in interpreting these dramatic events. All he would have to do was read them, all there in the past perfect tense.

A tall man in a long coat introduced himself politely, though he did not need to since Shun recognized him as a key and very public member of the central party's policy-making bureau. Over his shoulders, Shun could see the shapes of two other men standing in the background, away from the light.

I can only stay a minute, the bureau member said, *let's not waste it on ceremony. From your broadcast tonight, we were worried about you.* He paused, letting his message enough time to settle. Then he asked, *Have you been wondering what's happened to the students?*

No, I don't think so.

Do you think like your neighbors that some students have disappeared? That the PLA is responsible?

No, I didn't know my neighbors thought that. I didn't even know there were any soldiers.

Those are only irresponsible rumors uttered by peasants. You have done a famous job on television, and we want to encourage and help you. Then he flashed open his long coat.

Its folds were lined with sheets and sheets of stamped official papers. *Here,* he said, removing a set from the left side and handing it to Shun, *Here,* he said again, *this will help you understand our deliberated position. This is your new definite dogma on disappearance. But there's no need to read it, it's official,* he added. *It says that information transmitters are forbidden to convey stories about disappearances, ever. They're demoralizing; they can panic the people and destabilize the government. Besides, it's not true; it's not scientific, people don't just disappear.*

They both stood there a moment thinking about what had just been said. Shun could hear a man outside his apartment thumbing a butane cigarette lighter, *click, click, click,* before it was lost in the sound of another passing siren, before that too was replaced by a soft but distinct knocking on his door.

I must go now, the bureau member said and shook Shun's hand.

After he left, Shun continued standing in the middle of his apartment until the official papers dropped forgetfully from his hand. He then spent the rest of the night in a living room chair thinking about what the bureau member had said. Was his visit a warning? It definitely was not a routine visit announcing a policy change—that would surely have gone to the station manager or news director. Anyway why me, he thought. I just read the news that's handed to me ten minutes before I go on the air. Did I betray something when I read the student story tonight? And soldiers? And disappearances? There was no mention in the script. Besides, how would one read a story about disappearances, after all? What would be its effect? And who would believe it? Who can authenticate it, Shun asked himself, until he remembered some stories he had read in a gray-market American newsmagazine one day when he was waiting for someone in a downtown joint-venture hotel lobby, some stories about people disappearing in green Ford Falcons in Argentina and others losing themselves in Los Alamos, New

Mexico just before Japan surrendered in 1945. But maybe these were not the same things. Maybe, just maybe, he repeated to himself until it was beginning to get light outside.

The news director was not in his office when Shun went to see him the next morning. All of the drawers of the news archivist's filing cases and desks were opened however, overflowing with papers, as if someone had been trying to stuff them back into their files. Shun picked up a sheet from the many that were scattered on the floor. *Dateline Buenos Aires, August 7, 1977. Disappeared today, Pepe, Marianna and Angela Mendoza, father, wife and daughter, 27, 24 and infant, witnesses said, whisked away in a green Ford Falcon while they were walking along Avenida Florida in broad daylight. No known political activism or membership.* Shun picked up another one, another, a similar disappearance, Shanghai 1937, then Selma 1966, Warsaw 1945, and on and on, the room full of it, until he got to Hiroshima and Nagasaki 1945.

Dazed, he walked into the lobby and did not see anyone there at all, only gaps where they should have been. When he started out the sliding glass doors of the station building, he noticed too that everything on the outside had entirely disappeared, all of Beijing had absolutely vanished, except for his exact double, another Shun Min, walking up the sidewalk to the building as if it too had disappeared. He knew this to be true, he said to himself, because he could tell his story now in the first person, to an American stranger who had come to Beijing to teach translation to his niece.

(I met Crazy Shun shortly after the crackdown on Tiananmen Square on June 4, 1989, in the downtown apartment of a friend who had arranged for my teaching appointment in Beijing months ahead of its political spring, which I accepted against the travel warning of the U.S. Department of State. In our conversation that lasted well into the evening, he was very forthcoming about his duplicity in the media dissemination of news about the student unrest, and his brief encounter with the state security apparatus. For his protection, the details of his story and position have been altered to fit the narrative shape of this interview. He remained the model voice of China Central Television and Radio news well into the 1990s.)

COMING INTO BEIJING, 1997

for Moling

Don't tell anyone this
But I feel as if I'm coming home
Grass browning, coal smoke drifting
In this even November sunlight

Concrete block buildings in all colors
Dark figures in narrow *hutongs*
With less than a little money to spend
They have been here for generations, sweeping

Everywhere the carefully planted trees
Tendered rows of elms, willows and locusts
Above them the flitting magpies and higher
Always the crows that have witnessed all

And all have come to this, like me
Stones and people from every province
Still able to be astonished
Still doing wrong or right in different directions

Did I arrive with the right currency?
And enough cigarettes for everyone?
Unlike the Hong Kong I've just left
My Chinese is better understood here

The familiar, differing warm expressions
Their all-day tea jars warming in the sun
In the shadow of another Mao talisman
Or any other remediable mistake

I enter the city writing this poem
That has become important to remember
Holding back tears the entire ride
A 30-km trip I used to bicycle every weekend

At every intersection hundreds of bicyclists
Negotiate past truckloads of cabbage
Testament to another government surplus
Distributed free to every work unit

The same traffic signs are still cautious
Saying the exact same thing to cyclists
And the working horses that have refused
To pay attention for centuries in their toil

Next morning I will watch early dancers
Face the rising sun at the pavilion
As if they've just jumped out of prison
Onto the back of a dragon vexing everywhere

Early next morning I will also pick up
A fallen ginkgo leaf, wipe off the dew with my fingers
And press it deep into my passport
So dear, where it will stay, where I am not

PROFESSOR LI AT BRIDGE

Professor Li is a world expert on tea. I first met him in 1989, shortly after the Tiananmen Square incident when he was my partner in my first game in Beijing. That night we played in his university laboratory, trying to communicate—my Chinese was overwhelmed by everyone else's limited English—munching on peanuts and drinking tea out of lab beakers.

To make the game more competitive and challenging, they introduced me to a mini-IMP table combining the high card points of both hands, against which our raw score was compared. The resulting points were allocated accordingly. For instance, if my partner and I were vulnerable and held 27 HCP between us, and our contract was a meager 2NT making four with a raw score of 180 when the table shows that we should make 630, our opponents would get 9.4 mini-IMPS (MIMPs). [As a courtesy to bridge-playing readers, this unique mini-IMP table appears at the end of this chapter.]

That first game was mostly a very pleasant, social occasion, and I was not particularly upset when he opened a NT holding a singleton club, the ace, not even when he repeated it two hands later. After much persuasion, later that fall he promised me that he would never do it again. But even so, whenever he opens NT today eight years later, I hesitate and look up at him, sometimes raising the scowl of tournament opponents.

Over these last eight years we have played together quite a bit, in his lab and in Beijing tournaments. Whenever I'm in town, he has a game waiting for me. His English and my Chinese have improved, and our conversations have graduated beyond the eighth-grade level.

He is from the southwest and likes hot, spicy Sichuan food, the more peppers the better. As an intellectual during the demented Cultural Revolution of the 1960s, he was punished and exiled to the countryside for "thought rehabilitation." Upon his return, he found the lab he had designed and built had been totally trashed, his irreplaceable specimens along with all the equipment.

Despite all of this difficulty, Professor Li does not harbor anger or bitterness. The evening after he had told me about his nightmare experiences with the Red Guards, I saw him out dancing with his wife as well as most of the other women, his shock of white hair flowing the music across the ballroom. In the eight years I have known him, his only negative comment was directed at the younger Beijing tournament players, whose abrupt and rude behavior earned them his label of "hooligans" or "gangsters," as I translate the word from the Chinese.

Only semi-retired from research and teaching at 70 today, Professor Li is still warm, generous, sensitive, dignified and affectionate. When I saw him in Beijing a week ago, he informed me that his doctor wasn't too optimistic about his health, that he's had to substitute a moped for his bicycle, and that he can't go swimming with his grandson or dance any more.

His bridge game, at least for that night, did not seem affected by his declining health. Playing teams, on the second hand out he passed holding ♠ KQT ♥ Q73 ♦ K5 ♣ J543. After a 1 ♠ opening to my right, I doubled with ♠ 4 ♥ AK52 ♦ 9832 ♣ A876. After a pass to my left, Professor Li jumped to 3NT, a contract doubled by opener's partner. Luckily for us, the opponents did not find a diamond opening lead or switch. A spade was led to Li's ten and he played low club from his hand, winning the king with the ace. He played a low club from both hands on the way back, and the ♣ Q fell on air. Hearts broke 3-3, so Professor Li came home with plus 750.

Although his bridge is not particularly strong, I have enjoyed playing with Professor Li for his company and his friendship.

His bidding on the next deal was equally aggressive, or exceptional, depending on one's viewpoint. He held ♠ T653 ♥ T852 ♦ 86 ♣ AQ4. As South, I held ♠ K ♥ AQ974 ♦ A ♣ K97652. Both sides were vulnerable.

West	North	East	South
	Li		Me
2 ♦ (1)	Pass	2 ♥ (2)	Dbl (3)
3 ♠	Pass	Pass	4 ♠
Dbl	5 ♣	Pass	6 ♥

(1) Multi-colored opening, can be weak hearts or spades, or 4-4-4-1 hand (any singleton) with 16-19 HCP or two other options.

(2) Showing a poor hand and asking opener to clarify his hand.

(3) Hearts.

With a ♦ K lead, I made 12 tricks (West had the singleton ♥ J, so I needed to be in dummy twice for finesses, but clubs broke 2-2). After the round I asked Professor Li about the 5 ♣ bid. He looked at me and said, "You pushed me. You play hand. I know you can make 5 ♥. 5 ♣ asks you to choose heart or club slam."

At the table I believed him, and we won the match easily. Away from the table he tells me the best tea in China is grown on Hainan Island, and to make the best tea, the water should not be higher than the boiling point. I have learned to believe that too.

The mini-IMP table

	VUL	NV
20	0	0
21	50	50
22	100	100
23	150	150
24	300	200
25	450	300
26	600	400
27	650	450
28	700	500
29	750	550
30	800	600
31	900	650
32	1000	700
33	1250	850
34	1400	1000

35	1500	1100
36	1750	1300

To score:

Add total HCP from both hands

Look up score from table

Multiply the difference by 2 and divide by 100 for the MIMP

If difference is greater than 600, score is 12 + 1 for each 100 over 600

Example 1: Vulnerable

Total HCP = 27

Your contract is 2NT making 4 for score of 180

Table score reads 650

Difference is 650 − 180 = 470

(470 x 2) divided by 100 = 9.4

Opponents get 9.4 MIMPs

Example 2: Vulnerable

Total HCP = 34

Your contract is 3S making 7 for score of 260

Table score reads 1400

Difference is 1400 − 260 = 1140

(1140 x 2) divided by 100 = 22.80

Opponents get 22.8 MIMPs

Example 3: Vulnerable

TCP = 34

Your contract is 7S making 7 for 2210

Table score reads 1400

Difference is 2210 − 1400 = 810

(810 x 2) divided by 100 = 16.2

Your side gets 16.2 MIMPs

MADAME ZHOU'S PIANOS

When Madame Zhou Guangren opened the door to her apartment to greet us, one never would have suspected that she is one of the two most revered and honored concert pianists and piano teachers in China in the last century, for that matter, in all of Chinese history up to this point. (The other is Fou Ts'ong.) She was astonishingly gentle, gracious, authentic, clearly open to new possibilities in life and energized for this meeting. Definitely not the stuffy, vain and arrogant internationally-recognized musician and celebrity most others would be with her accomplishments. She was entirely comfortable and fluent in the English she had learned as a child in Germany where her father studied engineering, and later in Shanghai schools, making my accompanist more a witness than an interpreter.

I was there to present a copy of my 1997 novel *Chinese Opera* to her, a copy I borrowed from a Beijing friend for this occasion that had not been anticipated. This novel had been prompted by a story my piano teacher—a fine teacher and musician whose mouth was just honest enough to keep him from getting tenure in a music department in an American public university, Washington State University—told me about her before I went to China in 1991 as a Senior Fulbright Scholar. In it Madame Zhou appeared as herself in the same name, hosting the main character, a young Chinese American hotshot pianist teaching for the year in her piano department at the Central Conservatory of Music in Beijing. That was all fiction, that is, it was entirely made up in my imagination. When the novel was completed in 1992, Madame Zhou disappeared entirely from my imagination and my life.

She unexpectedly reappeared when I was visiting Beijing in May of 2007, in a taped interview on CCTV-Channel 6. Though I did not understand more than half the words of the interview in Chinese, I knew it had to be she, comfortable in her scoop-necked, simple red dress and a white, rope necklace, eyes that did not deceive or manipulate, her hair in broad curls. The host of the interview was clearly awed by her stature and, and there is no other way to describe this, her love of life. I watched the rest of the interview, more than an hour, transfixed by the television set as if I understood every word, which I didn't, and did. When the program was over, I picked up the phone and dialed a former student, Sophie, and asked if she was resourceful enough to find Madame Zhou in Beijing and arrange for this meeting. She accepted my hurried explanation and urgency for this most unusual request without question, as if her nine-year-old daughter Sarah who had been taking weekly piano lessons for the last two years made it easier for her to understand.

Dressed informally in a red top and basic-black slacks and embroidered house slippers, she led us into her living room full of CDs and VHF performance tapes wall-to-wall, ceiling-to-floor. Looking up after I had changed my street shoes to the slippers she provided, I saw the world's largest bottle of Johnnie Walker Red Label scotch whisky, the gallon size, unopened on a table in the kitchen behind her, maybe a present from an adoring fan.

We sat down and I thanked her for this audience and explained my reason for requesting it, to present her a copy of the novel *Chinese Opera* I had very carefully wrapped in red paper, the traditional Chinese color of giving, I remembered that much. "You are one of the main characters in this novel," I said. She opened it slowly, her eyes the ever gleeful and excited teenager, but cautious and patient enough not to tear the paper. That was when I saw her right hand, the fourth finger an inch shorter than the two on either side of it. The tape removed, she slipped the book out carefully, looked at the cover and opened it to two or three pages, set it aside, smiled at me and said in perfect English that she could not wait to read it that night.

Before I gave her the second present, also wrapped in red art paper, I was worried she already had a copy of the Deutsche Grammophon recording of Martha Argerich playing Robert Schumann's *Kriesleriana* on her shelf, maybe more than one copy. I had selected this piece because my novel's main character Sonny Ling had performed it in his conservatory recital for which Madame Zhou had provided the introduction. At the mention of *Kriesleriana*, the eighty-year-old Madame Zhou almost jumped out of her chair, her eyes filled with excitement. It turned out it was the piece she played when she took first place in the 1956 Schumann Competition in Zwickau, Germany, which of course I did not know. When I mentioned Martha Argerich, all she could say was "Martha, Martha, Martha, yes, 'born to play the piano'" she repeated, almost tearing the wrapping paper. Then she had to repeat several times over to convince me that she really did not have this 1990 recording and was not just being polite to a guest bearing gifts, like the one who had brought her that gallon bottle of Johnnie Walker Red.

I asked her what year she had her accident. 1982. With a colleague, she was moving a Steinway concert grand from backstage to the front for a visiting pianist's recital when the wooden pin holding the leg in place at her curved end of the monster slipped out, causing the leg to collapse and putting the suspended weight of the piano entirely on her two hands. She held it up as long as she could, her colleague frozen in horror, until it was just too much for her and it slowly crashed down, trapping her right hand underneath. Her colleague quickly threw a dirty handkerchief over this hand and rushed her to the nearest hospital in a taxi.

That had occurred in the spring, on an Earth First day when almost everyone in Beijing was out planting tree seedlings. There were few left at the conservatory that morning, few taxis in the street, and even fewer personnel at the hospital. The woman doctor on emergency duty who did not know music and who had never heard of Madame Zhou unwrapped the dirty handkerchief and said immediately that all three fingers would have to be amputated between the first and second joints. Here Madame Zhou stiffened her left fingers into a saw and demonstrated this terminal procedure with a surgeon's objectivity. No *ifs* about that! But when the doctor heard that Madame Zhou was a pianist, she took a different view.

"She then did a very funny, funny thing," Madame Zhou repeated and smiled that she had used the word *funny*, whispering it again to herself. First the doctor sent someone back to the conservatory to retrieve the missing tip of the fourth finger under the concert grand. When it arrived, she sliced off the piece of tissue under its nail, cut it into two, and grafted them onto each of the other two damaged finger tips missing their nails and the issue underneath. "'So the nails will grow,' the doctor explained." Then she gathered the crushed bones together tightly and bandaged them up before severing the last digit of the fourth finger that was beyond repair. "The doctor then said if there's no infection in the next two days, those fingers will be okay."

Luckily for Madame Zhou and for us, there was no infection. All three fingers healed, albeit the fourth an inch shorter at the last knuckle. Determined to play the piano again, she then devised a rehabilitation program for herself. Because she found it very painful to even touch the white keys on a piano with those three fingers, she put on a latex glove and played Chopin's "Berceuse" as softly and slowly at first as if it were the lullaby its title meant it to be. Here she hesitated a moment to catch her breath and the memory of these last details. Then she said that she played this piece for six months and nothing else, nothing. Not recognizing it by name, I asked if I could see the music for this magic piece. She went into the next room, but came back five minutes later empty-handed and said she could not find a copy of it in all of her Chopin music. I said that I would look it up as soon as I got home to America that weekend.

I explained that my teacher's version of this story was a bit different. The year was 1968 or thereabouts, not 1982, almost at the beginning of China's Cultural Revolution, he said. The Red Guards had shut down music schools as part of the teenagers' revenge-rebellion against authority, culture, the academics, and eventually each other. A period of national aberration, Chinese intellectuals now refer to that decade. As its consequence, Madame Zhou had to move a piano by herself, thereby causing this accident. How the geopolitics of the Cold War prevented people from getting the narratives right, the other's as well as our own.

She brought out tea for us, and fine, creamy chocolates, as well as some dry roasted walnuts and green raisins that she had just brought back from a distant western province where she had adjudicated. "You must eat them together," she explained and demonstrated how to do it by sandwiching the quartered walnut between two flattened raisins. They were delicious.

Getting her career back on track after this accident, she opened a piano school for children, and was quite successful at it for ten years, her instructions de-emphasizing the conventional high-finger position technique and focusing instead on using the weight from the shoulders and arms. Until she grew tired from teaching young, new students. With new piano studios springing up all over Beijing then, she explained, indeed all over China at the beginning of the 1990s, some charging huge sums of money, she decided to go back to the Central Conservatory of Music where she is still teaching full-time today to both graduate and undergraduate students, at the age of eighty.

We talked music next. Madame Zhou mentioned that at her most recent recital with an orchestra in Germany she played Mozart's 488. I thought it might have also been the last Mozart concerto I had played, but I was not sure about its Köchel number, and knew it only as No. 20. I tried humming it to her, but my humming was not recognizable by her, or me, and Sophie in fact gave me a frown. So we went into her studio to look at the music. Why not! My novel's character Sonny Ling had dinner here in Madame Zhou's apartment when she had quizzed him about the program he was practicing for his recital. Why can't the creator of that scene go into her studio!

And there it was, the nine-foot Steinway grand in a room whose built-in shelves were filled with sheet music on two walls. She went straight to the Mozart concerti section and pulled out several copies from a red-edition collection. No, I had played the 466, but the No. 20 was right. Hers in A, mine in D; major for her, minor for me; a common *allegro assai* movement, though in a different order. She said she really liked Alicia De Larrocha on the 466. So did I, with a copy in my car when I travel, but I just could not bring myself to mention it. Too many coincidences between fiction and reality already.

She pointed out some photographs on the shelves of her two children, a handsome son who also teaches piano at the same conservatory, and a daughter, and three grandchildren. There were pictures of numerous former students including one from the Caribbean, posing individually or in small groups, some informal, some at the piano, and some receiving awards. There was also a photo of Madame Zhou with Van Cliburn taken when she had adjudicated at his international competition held every four years at Fort Worth, Texas. There was a studio upright in her office in the adjoining room. As far as I could tell, there was no bedroom.

We went back to the living room. Sophie and I looked at each other and knew it was time to leave.

Madame Zhou accompanied us down the elevator from her fourth-floor apartment and walked us to the door. As we drove away in the rain, we waved at each other. She will soon begin preparing for her next recital, a two-piano, four-hands concert in Taipei next spring. I wanted to wish to be there for her performance, but in my mind is perhaps enough. That is the strength of fiction. As my friend Simon Ortiz has said, "If it's fiction, you better believe it."

EXIT, A CHINESE NOVEL

No one has been to Beijing
Without a visit to Tiananmen

Crazy Shu wrote these seemingly harmless lines forty years ago at the end of the war, when he was yet a teenager. It was October 1, and still wearing the remnants of a soldier's uniform and drenched in the tears of hope in Tiananmen Square, he stood under the yellow and red banners surrounding Mao Zedong's proclamation of an emancipated nation, the People's Republic of China. Then a young poet from Yunnan Province, he could have said the same thing about a visit to his Ruili River. But this was 1949, and Chiang Kai-shek had just fled to Taiwan with all of China's cultural treasures, gold reserves, and Steinway CDs.

Two years later Crazy Shu became Mao's special emissary, traversing the country giving poetry readings and encouraging younger writers, occasionally arbitrating canonical disputes among scholars and party officials. At his very last meeting with Mao in early 1976, Mao glued a poem to his heart: *If the world is round, then everything will eventually come to the same point.*

Crazy Shu never married, but hung on to all his things, both new and broken. After Mao's death that September, he was appointed a deputy to the Minister of Broadcasting, Film and Media, and assigned as principal speech writer for select members of the party's central committee. His mental notes accumulated between the lines of these printed speeches while he ignored their public reading—a disgruntled literacy against the state-owned telecaster echoing the number of words in each utterance and counting those in attendance for the evening's local news.

Secretly he did not believe that these hyper-real speeches could change anyone's mind, even if they were required reading at the mandatory weekly political study meetings at all levels in the nation. As the leader of his department, too, he was aware that as much as his writers wanted to, they could not believe what they had written. On those occasions when he visited some factories in Beijing to see how these speeches were being received, he noticed that the fastest readers had been selected to read them to a post-lunch audience half dozing and half reading something else tucked down in front of them. After one such visit, during which he saw that the unit's party leader was reading from the factory's World War II evacuation manual since the printed speech had not arrived on time, he contemplated starting a rumor that would eliminate these meetings.

But in fact, after the Tiananmen Square incident this year, these required meetings doubled. Crazy Shu was in the western provinces during the spring, and did not even hear of the event until his return in late June. As he was being driven back and forth on Changan Boulevard to learn what he could from the intervals between the recently-scrubbed stones, he was tempted to ask the driver to stop and let him out. But school children and tourists from Shanghai and Japan were there posing for pictures between the lions at Tiananmen Square, the Gate of Heavenly Peace, so he thought better of disturbing their play and privacy for the sake of what by now was perhaps nothing more than empty curiosity, so he thought.

Instead, he thought there comes a time when something happens that so totally devastates one's perceptions of hope, belief and act, that instinctively and personally one knows that he cannot live like that in that country anymore. He remembered his commemorative poem about the successful revolution forty years ago, and how free of censors he had felt in writing it. But in these recent years he has come to believe that poetry holds too much shelter for misfired metaphors and indulgent lies, and that, that is the real toad, he repeated. Even with censors and informants all around him, he was beginning to believe that fiction can better get at the exposed nerve, however elusive and transient. This time, not trusting poetry anymore, he defected into the beginning of the first story he was writing.

"If you forget who you are, or do not recognize yourself in your photos, you can look at their numbers. One survives by realizing that you can re-imagine it."

So Crazy Shu pretended to take the Ministry's next assignment in Stockholm, but already he was doubting that he can change anything leading the life of a refugee, a DP. What can he do with his spare time besides get up every morning and try to survive the day? *Tell me!* he pleaded with me as well as with himself. Learn to play rueful violin and look for a quartet to play with every Thursday evening? Give poetry readings as a dissident writer and rely on the generosity of PEN International or Harvard's Nieman? String for the CIA?

At Shanghai, where passports and exit visas were checked for the last time, Crazy Shu thought he recognized an odor in the airport concourse as something familiar from his Ruili childhood, but he wasn't sure it wasn't just unfinished presswood from another past or his imagination. From Hong Kong's Kai Tak airport, foreign faces started appearing in his British Airways 747. Some read the Bible for the first time, and some listened to a Romanian student who was at the Palace Square say, "I do not believe in good or bad communists, just communists. They are all crooks."

Now Crazy Shu put away his story he had been writing, and looked out of the cabin window from 30,000 feet. Remembering the exiled Cubans in Miami and Chinese on Taiwan, he thought that symbolic expatriation was seldom an option, and effective even less—though it had mattered to him that he had never been given the chance to give the heart of his heart, that the rest of his life might be worse than what he was leaving behind—and wondered if the real China will ever stand up.

(Crazy Shu was actually one of my older translation students in Beijing in 1989 who rarely came to class, but would wait for me outside the department building and engage me with his narrative about wanting to be a crazy writer, his words. Occasionally he would show me pages and pages of his manuscript, in both English and Chinese, in which he imagined himself as a protagonist in a novel exiling himself from China, as reconstructed in this imagined interview.)

Section 2

Crossing Cultures

THE GREAT WALL, AL, FLO, ZEKE AND ΔΔM

Having been in Beijing for less than thirty-six hours, I boarded a van headed northwest out of the inner city to tour the Great Wall with three other Americans, teachers assigned to Beijing Forestry University. The landscape was mostly agricultural along the one-hour drive up a winding mountain highway to Badaling, the North Pass at a strategic divide.

Over the last thirty-five years, the Central Committee of the Party, the ruling unit within the central government, developed several national plans to feed its peoples and make the nation self-sufficient in food production. The segment of the plan that applied to Beijing, China's capital, as well as most other Chinese cities, mandated that these individual municipalities in turn be self-sufficient in their food supply. As a consequence, Beijing city planners limited industrial growth, halted new heavy industry, and shifted to autonomous food production even as the city continued to sprawl outwards at an alarming rate.

Of the 9.5 millions people living in this area the size of Belgium and slightly larger than the state of Connecticut, 42 percent of its population is tied to agriculture. Strips of mostly deciduous trees, willows, poplars and other fast-growing softwoods, formed corridors separating the highway from the farms which, that early September, were harvesting a wide assortment of melons, grapes, apples, pears, corn, squashes, zucchini, waxed beans, peppers, potatoes, and tomatoes. Cattle and sheep grazed the hillsides, and hogs and chickens bivouacked at every bricked farmhouse, however small.

Horse-drawn carts transporting produce south and building materials north competed with the Mazda for use of the highway. As in the inner city itself, there appeared the non-ending development and construction activity all along and away from the highway. The obvious oversupply of manual labor seemed to be delicately balanced against random mechanization and automation. Individual workers appeared intent on small and isolated projects of independent labor with no apparent connection to any larger geography or engineering plan, an image difficult to visualize or even imagine in Japan.

But somehow the jobs get done here, always, the connections made, with or without the plumb line. Like the downtown traffic where there was no appearance of any regulation for the operation of cars, buses, trolleys, bicycles, farm tractors, animal-drawn produce carts, trucks and pedestrians—or if there was, no one paid any attention to them or enforced them, including the uniformed, smoking policemen standing on street corners— the users of this mountain highway were equally attentive, though they did not appear to be—to each other's space and movements while staying in constant motion themselves. The only consistent traffic covenant involved vehicles with wheels, which mostly used the right side of the streets and were generally attentive to the few traffic lights some of the time. It was pretty amazing to apprehend this chaos and realize that in Beijing at least, individuals arrived at their destination of choice on time and with fewer headaches, curses and accidents than their compatriot commuters in Los Angeles, Rome, London, Providence, or Tokyo.

On an occasional bridge stood a solitary soldier helmeted and armed with an AK47 at white-gloved, port arms position, his stare fixed at a frozen point over one's shoulder. His uniform was shaded the same green as Beijing's city police, its epaulets and shoulder patches differentiating their purpose and function. Their presence on these bridges seemed to reflect more particularly a Sandhurst perimeter containment mentality than a modern political philosophy.

At Badaling, the recently expanded northern city limits of Beijing, there were no soldiers or police (except as tourists themselves) guarding the Great Wall that was an idealization to keep out invaders from the north, at least according to some local historians. That the wall itself has actually kept anyone out, or in, is highly debatable, although dissident intellectuals tend to see it as a geographical symbol of internal oppression and cultural isolation. Legend has it that if and when The Wall is to fall, as sections of it did during the Cultural Revolution when the People's Liberation Army tore it down to recycle the bricks for barracks construction, the last soldiers will be instructed to send up smoke signals from treated wolf dung so that the turret guards at the Imperial Palace some forty-five kilometers south in the center of Beijing can prepare themselves for some serious combat. Legend also has it that in the first three centuries of the modern calendar, unwanted residents from the inner city were expelled through these gates at Badaling to face the *wolves of the terrifying wild west*. Modern legend records that The Wall is the only human edifice visible from the moon.

Reading about these legends in guidebooks had not prepared me for what I encountered. Traffic-directing policemen that the locals call *White Mice* augmented the tiny set of traffic lights at the narrow baluster which is itself part of The Wall, directing the endless flow of Toyotas, Peugeots, Mercedes, Red Flags, Volgas and even some Morris Minors through the north-south portal. The pigeons that have almost entirely disappeared from Beijing because of an extensive extermination program that seemed to have strayed to include other small birds by accident as well, now reappeared suddenly on the rooftops and building ridges north of The Wall, just as the trained homing pigeons that learned the political significance of the 28th Parallel and North Panmunjom and South Panmunjom during the Korean War truce talks at the border could tell discrete, arbitrary geographical differences. More than humans, they knew where home was, then as well as now.

The Wall here was built onto a ridgeback that appeared humanly not scalable from both approaches in most sections around Badaling. Started some 2,500 or 2,700 years ago, depending on which historian one talks to, more than a million pairs of hands and feet gave of their unpaid labor to its construction. At its initial stages before the advent of the modern calendar, those workers who died at this site, presumably prisoner-slaves, unwittingly also contributed their body parts as building material. During the Ming Dynasty, when Europe was trying to decide if Earth was round or flat or both and some actually ventured out to prove or disprove it or both, most of The Wall was refaced with stone and brick. Before and after this period, its history is blurry, as obscure as its real function and whatever else its metaphor may have represented in the Chinese imagination, as well as ours.

Today the government itself advertises The Wall as one of the world's greatest tourist attractions, like the Grand Canyon, the Eiffel Tower, or the Great Barrier Reef. And indeed, the only modernized cross-cultural tourist feature missing at this border site was access for the handicapped. There was piped music wired along sections of The Wall. The public toilets attended to by minority tribal teenagers collecting the five-fen user fee stood next to stores selling Great Wall postcards, *I climbed the Great Wall* t-shirts, Great Wall ashtrays, Great Wall satin pillows, Great Wall scarves, 1985 and 1989 Great Wall calendars hanging side by Great Wall side. There were also camels on which one could sit for Polaroid pictures, and ermine pelts at bargain price. Most of the tourists ventured west or east from Badaling, and some both.

Either direction is a climb, however, the western segment gaining some 400 meters in less than one kilometer. Most visitors seemed prepared with cameras, binoculars, water jugs, and for some, even four-course lunches with beer and fruit. It was odd that such organizing principles also included wearing suit and tie, volleyball uniform with Nike Air Jordans, spiked heels, legal briefcases, and a singularly beautiful older Mongolian woman with a floor-length, deep-blue native skirt with braided red trim interrupting this cognitive dissonance. She did not take notice of the young lovers on holiday from Shanghai snapping each other's picture on the high parapet in their matching Reeboks, but continued in her effortless stride up the steepest section of The Wall.

Stretched out 2,400 kilometers against an ecosystem of black pines, yews, sub-alpine spruces, dwarf oaks, mountain maples and white-spotted pines, The Wall must be the ultimate dream surface for the graffiti junkie. Only recently have the authorities begun a campaign to discourage graffiti art and smoking on The Wall. Most of the writing is in Chinese, but an occasional English or German word would appear. The first that caught my eye was *AL*, in four-inch block capitals. Then many steps later, *FLO*. Then *ZEKE*. Then ΔΔM, which I had to guess represented all the sisters in the Delta Delta Mu sorority at the University of Michigan. Then another *AL*. Perhaps it was carved by the same Al or same Al's girlfriend some 500 steps apart, or perhaps it was by another Al or his girlfriend, or perhaps it was by the first Al who had come up for a second visit and had forgotten he had already cut his name into a brick on his previous trip.

The fixed trope here is, of course, picture taking. Of each other mostly, and just maybe one frame left for the backdrop, the scenery, the landscape, the environment, the ecosystem, the other tourists, depending on how one looked at it. There were four cameras in my group of five, taking each other's pictures in various planned and random combinations. Such a camera stop took up at least ten full minutes. It was fortunate that I had not brought a camera along, since I had calculated that an additional camera in the group would have added at least seven more minutes into each camera summons.

The preferred pose while having one's picture taken at The Wall appeared to be perpetual détente. While courtesy seemed to be a rare encounter in Beijing's inner city as it is in all large cities, here in the high altitude, every possible courtesy is extended to the process of every individual picture being prepared and shot. No one, just no one, not even children, ventured into someone else's focal plane, regardless of how long it took to wait. If one listened carefully, one would have heard the three most frequently used words: *Yi, er, camera!*

On the way down I walked with one of the Educational Services with China teachers who was also taking notes. She was a fundamentalist or evangelical Christian, a recent master's-in-education recipient from the University of Virginia, who was in Beijing for the year to teach English to China's future foresters through the non-denominational, emphasized *non-*denominational, church organized and funded ESEC. She said this tour had been the happiest moment of her life, as she was able to experience history or myth, as I supposed one did by touring Manassas in Virginia, or Little Big Horn in Montana, or Heart Mountain in Wyoming, or the Lorraine Motel in Memphis. Legend has it that the former chairman Mao Zedong, China's modernization helmsman, had said, *If you don't make it to The Wall, you're not a Chinese.* Deconstructed by this member of the inter-denominational God-Squadder and applied to its mission, it meant, *Let's visit the Great Wall to see what being Chinese is all about*, whose subtext of course read, *Let me learn to love the Chinese, Lord.*

It is an ironic turn on this ultimate symbol of tyranny, that the individual lens can turn our planet's most visible matrix between order and chaos, good and evil, and incidentally, light and dark, as in ethnicity, into a delusionary experience of history just by being there for three hours, one of them spent squandering color nitrates. There may well have been human history here, some twenty-four or twenty-seven centuries of it, and I supposed it was even happening right then; but I didn't think that this was the kind of text that will be included in someone's focal plane, regardless of how long they stop to take pictures. For me, the moment has come to mean a collapsed sequence on seeing, after my descent from The Wall, a facsimile of my burgundy Jeep Cherokee in the parking lot, except I knew this one was made in Changchun in Jilin Province, and not Detroit, in the state of Michigan. For me, the moment has also come to mean the tall, dark Mongolian woman in blue visiting this matrix that was drawn to keep out her kin.

THE TEMPTATION OF CHINA

In 1989, the fortieth anniversary of the founding of the People's Republic of China, I taught poetry translation at a language center just a short bicycle ride from Tiananmen Square in Beijing. During a New Year's Eve party hosted by Ambassador James Lilley in his green polyester suit at the U.S. Embassy, I inadvertently insulted the career Foreign Service person in charge of the press and culture section. Two years later, I went to China as a Fulbright Lecturer, banished from Beijing by the same press and culture section to a remote key university in Changchun, in Jilin Province on modern maps, formerly Manchukuo, north of North Korea.

Since the 1844 Treaty of Wanghai, sponsored by President John Tyler to give American evangelicals the right to lease sites in five Chinese ports to construct schools, hospitals, churches and cemeteries, China had sent these missionaries packing five times in the 20th century: in 1900, 1912, 1919, 1927, and 1949. These repeated expulsions reflected both the indecisiveness of the Chinese government and the predatory interests of European and American economic and religious institutions in a flock of one billion. Now, however, the fundamentalist evangelicals were definitely back, quite possibly in larger active numbers in

Jilin Province than in my home state of Idaho, which houses Reverend Richard Butler's paramilitary headquarters of the Church of the Aryan Nation, as well as a number of people who had voted for George H. Bush again in 1992.

Greeting me at the university's foreigners' guesthouse were a Christian athlete and a freshly embossed B.A. from Texas, and a retired schoolteacher from Indiana, both without negotiable plans for a future career in the United States. Thus they had brought their mission to a country trying to define itself and move into the twenty-first century, its revolutionary and socialistic passion having anarchically degenerated into a passion for washing machines and blush. Now the country's young and sometimes disobedient included students who fell victim to these evangelical missionaries.

Little did I know that when Anson Burlingame brokered a treaty in 1868 between the Qing Court and the United States allowing the Chinese unrestricted rights of immigration, temporarily at least, and calling for American Christians to take their crusades to China because he believed it was ripe for missionaries "to plant the shining cross on every hill in every valley, for she is hospitable to fair argument," it would fast forward to my first Sunday in China as a Fulbright encountering a serious religious service in the next apartment, its singing and thumping rivaling the fervor of any revival gospel mission. I had left Idaho only a week before where conversion-doorbell terrorists ringing for Jehovah's Witnesses and other aggressive fundamentalist sects were unavoidable. There, at least I could say "Go away." Here the living room vibrated with the worshipping of unhyphenated white Americans. I walked downstairs into the courtyard where several other nonbelievers had gathered—a Jewish economist from Pennsylvania and two linguists from Wales. We looked at each other in shock, then huddled together in the apartment of the Welsh couple, listening to the deafening singing and stomping coming through the ceiling.

After our objections, we were promised that such services would be infrequent, and that they would warn us before they held another. These Fundies, or God-Squadders as they came to be known, conducted Bible studies with their students. I suspected these students exposed to foreigners for the first time in their lives were more eager to learn a foreign language than to have their souls saved, but I was never entirely sure. I was certain, however, that I could not trust the elasticity of such a symbiotic relationship.

Often I wondered if they had confused the meanings of missionary and mercenary. A non-Christian Georgetown University recent graduate that I knew said that her fifty-eight-year-old roommate Sally, a former military secretary now a born-again global crusader, had sold her Chinese-language cassette tape picked up free at the United States Information Agency. In her absence one day, Sally re-appropriated it and sold it again to another foreigner for a quiet, taxpayer-subsidized and tax-free profit of ¥ 135. In another instance, the Christian athlete exploited his teacher-student relationship by exhorting his students to give him free Chinese-language lessons because, as he reasoned, "They owe me. I'm the best thing they'll ever have in their lives."

Who were these semi-volunteer crusaders, what were they really doing in China, and why did the Chinese government welcome them?

Most of them were recent converts into these fundamentalist Protestant sects; most were either recent graduates under the age of twenty-five, or around sixty and recently retired from lifelong blue-collar or semi-professional service positions—in either case impressionable and vulnerable people themselves, ambivalent, uncommitted and uncertain about their economic futures in the United States. Those few between twenty-five and thirty-five were mostly administrators, many of whom had accepted a second two-year tour, putting off facing the cultural, political and economic realities of the U.S., hoping something would come together for them in one of China's larger cities. Occasionally something did. There was the teacher education major from the University of Virginia who left the fold after two years to accept a lucrative position as English language coach and copy editor for the three joint-venture Holiday Inns in Beijing.

With China becoming another international power, it is understandable that foreign language acquisition, especially of English and Japanese, has become one of its chief educational goals. Consequently the official responsibilities of the God Squad focus entirely on teaching English: reading, writing, and conversation, at both the undergraduate and graduate levels.

It is easy to understand why China welcomes these Fundies. They do not drink, smoke, swear, or mess around; they have some language and culture training, though most of their six-week orientation focuses on China's hygiene and foods, networking, and soul-conversion techniques; often they come with free teaching materials hard and expensive to find in China; with no linguistics training, they unquestioningly adapt China's outdated language curriculum and teaching methodology; having learned their own realities in the same way, they immediately bond to the forty-century-old learning by rote teaching pedagogy; and the government has to pay them only minimum teachers' wages and provide standard housing. Their sole vice appears to be chewing gum, which China already manufactures along with Coca-Cola, Marlboros and Jeep Cherokees. In short, as global flotsam they represent no political threat to either the Chinese government or cultural institutions. Even while China unilaterally canceled the Fulbright Program and most of the Sino-U.S. educational exchange programs in the fall of 1989, in retaliation to the U.S. reaction to the political spring of Tiananmen Square, it nevertheless allowed these fundamentalist teachers' language programs to continue— though it later expelled two such teachers for teaching Christmas carols in class at a military academy in Wuhan.

It is also clear that these quiet and unobtrusive spiritual purveyors have tacitly agreed to divide China into two zones, the Educational Services Exchange with China (ESEC) out of Pasadena, California, ministering to the southern flock; and University Language Services (ULS) out of Tulsa, Oklahoma, home of Oral Roberts University, the latecomers claiming the rural and colder north. Both ULS and ESEC claim their organizations are non-denominational, where inter-denominational would be more descriptive. Nevertheless, it is primarily through the networking of these two organizations,

Americans came to know about China, through these missionaries. For more than a century, the chief source of cultural information about China has come through similar missionaries, be it the semi-literate Southern Baptists or not-much-better Missouri Synod Lutherans. Were not Nobel laureate Pearl Buck's parents missionaries?

And for those few American readers who stumble onto *The New York Times* articles by the Pulitzer-winning Nicholas D. Kristof or Sheryl WuDunn, they will find these pages refusing to acknowledge this American missionary presence in China, let alone interpret the two-way impact of this cross-cultural phenomenon. (Here I am reminded of journalist Theodore White's battle while he was in Chungking covering WWII, with *Time* publisher Henry Luce born in China to Presbyterian missionaries, in which White is alleged to have said that nothing he writes will see print in the magazine.)

Walking with the Beijing coordinator of the ESEC to a state banquet for foreign experts and consultants held at the Great Hall of the People hosted by Premier Li Peng in the fall of 1989, I heard her remark how wonderful it was that China had eliminated homelessness and hunger in forty short years, and that she had not seen a single pregnant woman (the subtext meaning that China has at last controlled its population?) or heard a single car honk on the busy Changan Boulevard in downtown Beijing (meaning that the noisy Chinese have learned to reduce noise pollution?). I did not have the heart to tell her that her information had come from China's official and only English-language newspaper, *China Daily*, using cooked data supplied by the government's Bureau of Statistics, and that "No

Honking" signs in Chinese had been posted on Changan on both sides of the Gate of Heavenly Peace. Later when Li Peng went from table to table greeting all the guests in the 158-tabled banquet room in a contrived gesture indicating business as usual, Tiananmen Square or no Tiananmen Square, this ESEC coordinator refused to accept his toast, not even with Coke or OJ, reminiscent of John Foster Dulles' refusal to shake Zhou Enlai's hand in Geneva in 1954.

I find such political rejection girded by racist overtones. In 1991 there were about 150 ULS teachers and family members in Jilin Province, as well as six other American teachers, including another Fulbright, an economist from LaFayette College. The ULS held a Thanksgiving celebration in an upscale Changchun hotel, and invitations went out to all Americans in the province except me, a Chinese American, the only non-white in the group. Later I learned from the Georgetown graduate that "No Natives Allowed" had been printed on each invitation, using the same language as the signs that surrounded a park across Suzhou Creek in Shanghai's infamous foreign concession, "Chinese and Dogs Not Allowed," until the successful communist revolution trashed them in 1949. Nor was I spared the old colonial I-don't-see-you, you-all-look-alike dismissal in the perception of these missionaries who did not recognize me in public. The German male tourists and consultants in Beijing also ignored the Chinese, their looks particularly hateful when they saw me in the company of a white woman. The teachers referred to their students as *boys* and *girls*, even when all of their students were at least a decade older than they, a throwback to the nineteenth century's racist missionary and military use of linguistic representation and suppression. Their children further reflected such colonial outlook in their elitist, rude and dismissive responses to the natives.

*   *   *

In the late spring before I left Changchun, Bob, the retired Indiana schoolteacher with no economic future in the United States, whose Social Security was being challenged by his family, knocked on my apartment door. He asked if I would be bothered by another worship service in his apartment, which was adjacent to mine. The very next day the ULS provincial coordinator knocked on my door. "I understand you are writing an article critical of ULS—can we discuss this?" he asked. I told him I didn't think we had a common language to discuss this subject, especially when they insist that the ULS (and ESEC) is only a public-service organization rather than a religious one exploiting the teacher-student relationship in order to convert lost souls.

It has almost been a century since the Boxer Uprising when a dissident secret society unsuccessfully fought back the oppressive outrages of foreign powers trying to dominate China's politics, culture, economics and spirituality, having lost Hong Kong a half century earlier in the unequal Treaty of Nanking. Echoing the sentiments of Wang Lun and the White Lotus sect of another failed rebellion in Shandong another century earlier, the Boxers found their membership among farmers and workers who practiced the martial arts, meditation and herbal healing, and drew on a wide assortment of spirits and protectors. Acting on self-reliance and the inviolable domain of individual moral conscience, their primary targets of Christian missionaries and their Chinese converts led to their eventual suppression by foreign military power.

It is now 1995, and Hong Kong is being returned to the Chinese after almost a century of British colonial rule. I have just returned after another visit to China, struck by the media's reports of China's miraculous economic growth in the last two years. Ten percent. Thirteen percent. One as high as twenty-seven percent. What is being counted? Where is the count being taken? I certainly did not see much of it in the areas away from the coast and urban centers, and what I saw was contradictory and inconsistent, the wealth accumulating in the hands of a very few, many of them belonging to foreigners. There were more with less, and more having to work twice as hard as two years ago just to keep what they have. Yes, there were numerous cellular phones carried by businessmen wearing $299 Pierre Cardin ties dining at Maxim's in Beijing, but only feet away from a group of very young beggars. Yes, there were new department stores and fancy boutiques filled with consumer items, including gold-plated Hasselblads, but at the same time, teachers find that they have to work at more than one teaching job just to stay even, the Air Force has to operate resorts in order to meet its budget cutbacks, and universities have taken to running gas stations to balance their expenses.

This kind of economic instability and uncertainty usually disenfranchises certain groups of citizens, making them alienated and vulnerable, lost souls waiting to be saved. And yes, the evangelicals were still there, more visible and more active and in larger numbers, but this time accompanied by recent American and European graduates with business degrees looking for tax-protected investment and career opportunities.

Are the Chinese responding to the evangelicals because they want to use Christianity as a stay against rampant capitalism, or because they want to use Christianity to justify their temptation by capitalism? In Russia, television viewers are hounded by Snickers commercials and Christian conversion messages, which should of course raise the final question: Is the subsidized economic growth that is sweeping China today merely reflecting the most recent attempt by western nations to commit political, cultural, economic and spiritual genocide, to show that we have not lost China, that we can still save China? Or has China learned its lesson so well that it will best us at what we've been doing to it for centuries?

(1995)

AHEAD IN THE NL-EAST

C*hangchun, Jilin Province, China—China Daily*, which calls itself "China's national English-language newspaper" and is published simultaneously abroad in Hong Kong and New York, has been the only newspaper that I've read in about the three weeks since I left Moscow, Idaho.

Every other issue carries the previous day's major league baseball scores on its sports page, and twice in three weeks, the league standings, both American and National, along with the UK professional football results. The last I knew, my team, the Pittsburgh Pirates, was leading the National League East, ahead by about ten games with about twenty left to play.

But since it takes the newspaper about four days to get to Changchun—where the U.S. Embassy has assigned me to teach American literature for the year at one of China's key higher education institutions, Jilin University, best known for its chemistry and mathematics programs—the baseball news is quite out of date for a die-hard Pirate fan. I am reminded however that it took about the same amount of time for the Sunday *New York Times* to reach Brookings, South Dakota, where I faced my first and another challenging teaching appointment. Anything can happen with some twenty games left, although neither the

Cards nor the Cubbies have the talent this year to make that autumnal charge. [The Pirates won the division title, but lost to the Braves in the league playoff, as they did again in the next season.] Too often I forget that the newspaper is an exercise of cultural and economic power. Out of an accumulation of neutral, private and public acts, certain stories are carefully selected and politically framed for a generally innocent, uninformed and semi-literate reading public that believes it is getting the truth along with the *Prozac*. (As I write this, I am reminded of what a friend told me two years ago when I was reading *USA Today* everyday in Beijing, the only English-language foreign newspaper available in China in the days immediately following the Tiananmen Square incident, that it would be habit-forming and would definitely lead to my mental deterioration.)

That just about every daily newspaper in the United States regardless of the size of its community would six months of the year print the baseball standings and box scores of most if not all of the previous day's games, is unchallenged journalistic orthodoxy. That a newspaper omitting a sports section altogether, and hence driving at least the male portion of its readers to television, would bring outbursts from the National Education Association and Kevin Costner out to stump for literacy, and changing channels without a television, as they do in Santa Fe, is a certainty.

The truth is, I have grown to accept the prevalent journalistic convention in the United States. I expect my baseball scores today, and the *Idahonian/Daily News* and all the other hometown newspapers of places where I lived have satisfied my addiction that they had helped create. But what about the University of Idaho exchange students or faculty from Beijing whose sports interests focus on China's international performance in soccer, gymnastics or volleyball? Does the *Idahonian/Daily News* print these sports' results? Or are they just considered a minority reader in the wrong geography, like I will be for the next eight months?

What is the prevalent American newspaper editorial policy in the coverage of those public and private events that take place abroad, say in China? I am reminded that not a single American print journalist had a regular assignment in China prior to June 4, 1989, and that CNN was here to cover head of state of the U.S.S.R. Mikhail Gorbachev's visit to Beijing and fortuitously stumbled onto the political violence at Tiananmen Square.

Things are different now. It is 1991, two years since the Tiananmen Square incident, and the *Washington Post*, *New York Times*, *Los Angeles Times* and UPI all have stations in Beijing from which dispatches are regularly filed. Last week a story was faxed describing our congressional representatives Nancy Pelosi, Ben James and John Miller idiotically unfurling a black banner in front of the Monument to the People's Heroes at the center of Tiananmen Square to commemorate those Chinese students and intellectuals who had died for democracy two years ago. I would suspect that UPI carried this story, and that the *Idahonian/Daily News* ran it, as well as every single newspaper in Hong Kong and Taiwan.

But are these Chinese events as they are vetted and edited in American newspapers really different, or are they printing different stories but recycling the same American hegemonic and more than often racist view toward China and the Chinese? In the last two years, article after article has appeared in the big hitters—*Time, Newsweek, New York Times, Washington Post*—that focus on the human rights issue following Tiananmen Square, or the health condition of China's eight elderly leaders.

They often make uninformed conjectures about the future of China, reflecting the old bunker mentality's domino theory that if communism/socialism falls apart in eastern European countries and the Soviet Union, surely China will be next, surely China too will be rocked by this apparently worldwide collapse of socialism.

Focusing on the exaggerated political, religious or agricultural crisis, these speculative articles often make dramatic and lively reading, and the innocent American reading public has been led to believe that these Chinese leaders do not have enough prestige, influence and connection to wield that ultimate bastion of political power, self-perpetuation.

Did you read that another Chinese leader is on a heart support system? When Deng Xiaoping dies, will there be a power crisis or power vacuum, will he be replaced by a reformist or liberal, will the Communist Party lose the support of the People's Liberation Army (PLA), will the local police and the Public Security Bureau lose their ability to identify and suppress political dissidence, and will it be a sign that things are falling apart in China?

I happen to believe that the few American journalists stationed in China have been sending back a lot more stories than those that are published, that basically they are doing their job. It's their publishers who are selecting which ones to print, in the words of the editor of *Ms Magazine* Robin Morgan, "what the ad agencies and their clients insist that 'the public' wants to read."

And who assumes what the American public wants to read about China? Our North Carolina Jesse Helms who has described China as a rogue elephant that lies whenever possible? Perhaps not literally, but it does seem to accurately describe the publisher's hidden selection policy.

Tiananmen Square is over! It's two years old! It's not news anymore. Even the editors of the *Spokesman Review* were convinced that their readers were no longer interested in any story out of China as they rejected my request for press credentials. There are other stories today, including the authorities recently releasing most Tiananmen Square political prisoners and commuting the sentences of others, but unfortunately they have not hired a Hill & Knowlton to advertise this in the United States.

Our press would have us believe that the basic issue or contention between the United States and China is human rights. Even if this were a politically correct agenda, it is questionable why we are so strident and ideological in conducting our human rights diplomacy. Are we hiding something about ourselves in this posture? Are we beginning to believe in, and live by, our own myths about ourselves? About others?

In the meantime, the American public is not being informed about some major issues that the United States must work closely with China to resolve: bring China beyond the agreement-in-principle stage of nuclear non-proliferation, stop China's sales of the M-9 missile to Syria and the M-11 missile to Pakistan.

Get China to curb its sale of Norinco small arms and munitions on the global market, especially its folding AK-47s. Get China to participate in the global efforts to control missile technology and chemical warfare.

Open bilateral market access in China and encourage it to cease its unfair trade practices and trade deficit. Provide incentives for China to participate in the international intellectual and patent rights legal system. Develop a cooperative structure to monitor women's rights in China. Involve China in the global environmental movement.

It is little wonder, as uninformed as the American public is about China, that our government did get away with being aloof with China in the last two years, and basically did not carry on any kind of significant dialogue with it. In just the last week, John Major of the United Kingdom, Giulio Andreotti of Italy, Wee Kim Wee of Singapore and Nguyen Manh Cam of Vietnam have visited Beijing.

It is time that bilateral, mutually constructive talks between these two major global players be held at least at the level of the Secretary of State. (A reporter for the *Toronto Globe and Mail* told me at a Beijing reception two weeks ago that Henry Kissinger was recently seen in the capital sporting an Elton John hat, but he was here representing American private business interests this time, and not the State Department or the White House.)

So take note, Randy Frisch and Kenton Bird. [Editors of the *Idahonian/Daily news* in which this essay first appeared.] What stories about China are you selecting from the wires to print?

I don't think it's enough that your Palouse readers get timely baseball scores, and in fact suspect that most residents would give them up for a more representational selection of global reality. In compensation, until I take the cure, perhaps you could fax each Pirate divisional playoff and the World Series' scores to me, the same way that much of China received its news of Tiananmen Square two years ago.

WHO OWNS THE ENGLISH LANGUAGE?

Like its 1,092-page, seventy-four-year-old precursor—the 1925 *Oxford Book of English Prose,* edited by Sir Arthur Quiller-Couch—this new, heftier, and expanded version is a taster's tour of sample literary excerpts that reflect both the not-yet-knighted editor John Gross's sense of representative, major English language prose writers and their individual artistic achievement. Organized within a five-century chronological framework, from Thomas Malory (1485) to Kazuo Ishiguro (1995), the anthology provides an essential, useful, and obligatory reference compendium for students and readers interested in the history and evolution of English literary texts. Writers represented include both those who have selected to work within English as a second language by choice, such as Chinua Achebe, Joseph Conrad, Vladimir Nabokov, and Salman Rushdie, and those who wrote or write in English by default.

Perhaps the most significant expansion of this second anthology reflects the changing linguistic map of the use of English since 1925. While Quiller-Couch's selections included only fifteen American writers, for less than five percent of the total number of entries, Gross's inclusion of one hundred Americans, or twenty percent, indicates that for most of the twentieth century the English language has been used by a larger and more multinational community than merely the residents of England or Great Britain or the United Kingdom. Add to this the fifty writers Gross included who are not English or American, and one can easily see the irony of the problematic position faced by the American Mike Morrow, the publisher of Asia 2000 based in Hong Kong, who believes that English is a Chinese language because more people use it in Asia today than in the rest of the world combined.

For sure, critics will emerge to spar with Gross about the appropriateness of the included selections as soon as the ink hits the page, be they Donald Hall, Robert Pack, and Louis Simpson, joint editors of 1957's seminal *New Poets of England and America* (who got to share the punches), or Donald Allen, who challenged them with his 1960 *New American Poetry: 1945-1960* (and who had to endure the jabs by himself). This is an expected convention in the sport of constructing an authoritative and defining literary text, the precursor to the compilation of a reading list for what we are fed to read in the grade school, high school, college, and what the doctoral candidate in literature is examined on. Quiller-Couch, for example, shortsightedly omitted James Joyce and D.H. Lawrence.

While I have no quarrel with the individual selections in this new anthology, I am very uncomfortable with what appears to be the political underpinning of such criteria as *eloquence* (in its good sense), *literary merit,* and *fine writing* that colors the entire anthology: nineteenth-century *good taste.*

Air travel can often be a very disturbing experience when the person sitting next to me gets the true answer to the initial exploratory question, "What do you do?" I learned very early to start lying, that what I must not say is "I teach English," as this answer especially from an Asian has always choked my fellow passenger into a very uncomfortable, eyes-avoiding silence for the next two or three hours, after he or she first mumbles something about getting a "C" in it, whatever *it* is.

Presumably the silence reflects a wish not to be linguistically judged anymore, that the "C" received for mediocrity in language usage has expanded into a refusal to participate in a conversation with a language cop—someone whose didactically prescribed norms for excellence (a.k.a. class) in using the language facilitate the acceptance of who we are in the present, evaluate our past, and hence cast a mold for our future. We in the United States do not need one of Prince Charles' regular pilgrimages to a shrinking dominion to remind us of the contemporary savaging of the English language. Our college composition classes make sure that linguistic models of good taste will be admired, mimed, and reproduced, at least by those students with a "B" or higher grade. Those with a "C" or lower, however—those who dare to introduce into their essays street idiom; unusual word choice; inventive word order; unique combinations of words; outright creative language experiments of the imagination—are muffled into silence. For the remainder of their lives, they not only make a point of avoiding *English teachers* but sadly also stay away from reading books that in fact reflect a more flexible and diverse use of the English language than what they were taught.

Too often, statements about language are fused with metaphors about God or Truth or Patriotism. The dust cover of this anthology asserts that "the full range of English prose... reveals a variety of achievement which no other language can match." Such an imperialistic and xenophobic position regards language as a set of sign systems that attempt to be God, pleasing the anglophile while ignoring the necessity of looking at language in all of its constant cultural interplay with class, gender, and ethnicity, in all its spikes and dips on the linguistic graph, not just in its filtered and buffed samplings.

For example, the William Faulkner selection is a set piece from *The Sound and the Fury* rather than a more ambitious excerpt from *Absalom, Absalom!* So, too, the Gertrude Stein selection comes from *The Autobiography of Alice B. Toklas* instead of something more daring from, say, *Wars I Have Seen.* (The James Joyce selections do include passages from both *Ulysses* and *Finnegans Wake*.)

Even the Tom Wolfe selection is relatively safe, from *The Bonfire of the Vanities* rather than from "The Kandy-Kolored Tangerine-Flake Streamline Baby" or "Mau-Mauing the Flak Catchers." And what about Wolfe's contemporaries such as Joan Didion and Hunter S. Thompson? And finally, where is the work of such writers as Ben Okri, Ishmael Reed, Gilbert Sorrentino, Maxine Hong Kingston, Cormac McCarthy, Carlos Bulosan, Robert Coover, N. Scott Momaday, and Joy Kogawa? Their inclusion might well have made this anthology more illustrative of the fuller range of writers who have both explored the diversity and extended the shifting boundaries of the English language.

"WHERE ARE YOU REALLY FROM?"

1.

Several years ago at a Howard Johnson's lounge in Oshkosh, Wisconsin, an anglo sitting at the bar next to me finished reading his *Wall Street Journal*, noticed me for the first time, and immediately fired his only mental association for me.

Where are you from?

He wasn't satisfied that I said I was from Boston first, then tried Pittsburgh, Galesburg, Iowa City, Brookings, or any of the other places I had a legal address. He wanted to know the truth.

Where are you really from?

How about an exchange student from North Vietnam? How about the last of the Shoshone in drag? One thing led to another, and the rest is a matter of public record.

2.

The Delores Mendoza of our activism are not the physicists and other clinical scientists whose resume is filled with government and foundation funded research projects, but their semi-colleagues, the American Asians in the humanities.

For they are the charley's of the dominant insipid, schizophrenic institutional orientalism against the Asians, wardens of a possessive, perverse, and pervasive hateful curiosity of the mysterious East that can be directly traced back to 19th century Britain when every titled lady had an Asian houseboy, or to Russia where Catherine the Great pressed shipwrecked Japanese sailors into professor of Japanese for imperial service, or to 19th century Baptist and Lutheran theft of Chinese orphans and antique furniture.

3.

(Hey, what's the matter with you. I have nothing against you. I like you people. During the war I fought for years against those dirty Japs, on your side. I love your country. All I want to know is where you're from. Originally.)

4.

The biggest enemy of our position are the academic Asianists. The professors of economics. Of political science. Of history. Of Chinese/Japanese civilization, culture, language, literature. Those *isei* and *nisei* scholars walking about our campuses wearing those ginsberg glasses long before the publication of "Howl."

5.

Ironically, as it always is with racism, they are among the worst victims in the anglo mind-fuck of us yellows.

6.

:they are politically naive and hence impotent, the concept of politics that they (choose to) see limited to those on the international level

:they have absorbed the dominant views about the arts, that is, their children should select some respectable profession other than those of a writer, composer, or painter/sculptor/ photographer

:they teach their children to avoid the browns, step around the reds, and be scared of and have the blacks simultaneously

7.

When their children meet each other in public, alone in a part of town unknown to them, and themselves unknown to each other, they look very quickly past each other. Avoiding any eye contact.

Or cross over to the other side.

Is it a shame to be yellow? To be seen by another yellow on a white street in a white neighborhood? To be seen at all?

Much sadness.

8.

(I wonder if I should really do an anthology of Asian-American literature. There is so little of it around that's any good. Let's see now, a few years back I did a bibliography for the MLA. Where did it go? I hope I didn't lose it; it took so long to research and compile. Here it is, in the small folder labeled Asian-American Affairs.

(Lawson Inada, Richard Kim, Alexander Kuo, Stephen Liu, David Wang. No more? Oh, that's right, I couldn't find any more.

(Well, my publisher wants me to do one. It won't be so difficult a task. There're very few writers around, so it'll be easy to look at all that's been published. Maybe some would even be grateful to get anthologized at all.

(What criteria should I use for making the selections? What sort of chapter introduction should I make? This is going to be the most difficult part, since known works by O'Neil, Faulkner, Melville, Pound, Stevens, etc., are so superior, so refined, especially T.S. Eliot.

(And where should I go to find all the works? None of the books have been left in print, and the rest are scattered mostly in small little's.

(Maybe some of my friends in Iowa City, Stanford, Amherst will help me out.

(Yeah, I'll do it. It'll be good for my career, being known as the Asian-American literature specialist. Or better still, as the one who discovered Asian-American literature.)

9.

The reason that the question "Where are you really from?" is racist follows:

1. the anglo's stereotyping of Asians as worshippers of antiquity is more a reflection of his basic inability and the lack of interest to know anything about Asians, especially Asian Americans

2. correspondingly, the anglo's knowledge of Asians, what little there is of it, is restricted to a very self-serving colonial view of its antiquity, and is a corollary of #1.

The point is this: for what cannot be efficiently assimilated into the anglo's cultural mainstream through such forms as the happy yes-boss Kono, or Dr. Cheng-is-one-of-the-most-respected-citizens-in-town and makes-his-race-proud, the rest is collected together into some cultural antiquated package to be opened away from the domain of contemporary political/social/cultural experience.

And this: if we keep on looking at Asian antiquity through such glasses, or at best at San Francisco's or Portland's Chinatowns while only thinking about its restaurants and curio shops, or at Seattle's while only thinking about the proposed baseball domed stadium, then we don't have to deal/live with the contemporary Asian American experience. In other words, we can then dismiss the issues faced by Asian Americans in the areas of crime, illiteracy, underemployment, aging, housing, particularly compounded since 1968.

10.

(Yes, the anglo is doing something for us. ((As if we ever asked for it.)) We are not ignored. We are not invisible. We have our bootstraps we can pull. They are interested in us. They ask about the use of the human figure in our Sung Dynasty landscape paintings. They ask us where we are really from. They care. They asked me if I knew Benny Wong from New York, just the other day.)

11.

Yes, Sung Dynasty painting. The Haiku. Geisha girls. Oriental literature translations. This type of ethnic exotica, known otherwise as ethnic vulturism, or ethnic voyeurism, or the sino-mentality, or the post-chinoiserie phenomenon, this *orientalism*, has always been a form of racism, and of the worst kind, since on the surface it pretends to be interested in the very culture it is stealing or destroying.

And worse, this kind of mind-fuck creates and sustains such disastrous thinking as Asia-has-no-present, Asia-has-no-science, Charlie Chan, Kung Fu, and Where-are-you-really-from-originally-because-I'm-innately-interested-in-antiquity-you.

12.

In other words, the thinking goes something like this: if the anglo cannot totally absorb the Asian American into its Pepsi-Evinrude-Racism-Sexism cultural mainstream, we Asian Americans will be allowed to carry out our cultural determinism as long as it takes place safely removed from having any impact on our anglicized day-to-day experiences.

In fact, our colleges and universities will help that system along, particularly with the cooperation of the academic Asianists. There will be programs inviting visiting professors to speak on landscape and the calligraphic arts, translators to speak on language and ancient verse (often with metaphoric or forked tongue, like the way Indian Joe and Cain talk in the movies), self-styled experts to demonstrate flower arranging and karate, and the know-it-all cultural *ah mahs* to cover 10,000 years of civilization in a single fifty-minute lecture.

And of course, everyone will be invited to a tea and shrimp with green peas dinner at the local panda restaurant, celebrating the release of the first WHERE-ARE-YOU-REALLY-FROM anthology by a major publisher.

13.

Our ancestors sure made a monkey out of you, ha, ha.

(1971)

CULTURAL CONFLICTS IN A CARD GAME

As an American Senior Fulbright Scholar assigned to teach American cultural studies at Jilin University in Changchun, I also managed to play competitive bridge in this cold region of China north of North Korea, formerly known as Manchuria or Manchukuo. A few days ago, I stumbled into the annual seven-day Jilin Province Team Championship. It was an experience to remember.

I had casually asked someone in the literature department at the university if there was organized bridge in Changchun. Within the hour, I received a telephone call at my apartment warning me to be ready—Shi Yi, a chemist, will be my partner, and he will be there in five minutes.

Shi Yi and I rode our bicycles to the huge game building where Go and Chinese chess are played in addition to duplicate bridge. During the ride over, I found out that we would be playing precision, Taiwan style. Beyond the handful of legal bridge words that he knows in English and I in Chinese, we had no linguistic communication.

The playing site was packed, with three times as many kibitzers as players. I discovered that in China kibitzers do not hesitate to reach over and pull out detailed hand records during the play, nor are they shy about commenting loudly on bids and plays—or about blowing smoke in the players' faces.

There were 56 teams in the event—more than expected—so there were not enough curtains and bid boxes to go around. Some tables used paper for recording the auctions.

Gradually I caught on. It was a tournament. Four rounds of 16 boards per day for seven days. Swiss teams with cumulative scores in Victory Points.

On the first set of the third day, we played against the only women in the event. We used paper to mark our auctions. Everyone at the table was very polite and smiling. Our opponents were playing Precision, but by now I had learned enough to know their version of Super Precision.

I heard 1 ♦ by dealer on my left. My partner overcalled 1 ♥. My right hand opponent passed. I held ♠ AT865 ♥ T95 ♦ QT2 ♣ A8. It was 8:20 a.m. and I've had bridge partners in America who would not get up until noon. I knew my partner had fewer than 16 high-card points (with more he would have doubled), and that we had a heart fit.

I also knew that opener might be short in diamonds. That's true even with Standard American players I encounter in Lewiston Idaho where I sometimes play in its club. Anyway, if we could bid game on this board, it might demoralize the opponents and give an edge for the next 15.

I bid 2 ♦. I didn't care how my partner interpreted the bid, but he did not knock on the table, which would have indicated an Alert for an artificial bid, although in Changchun as well as in Beijing, it is often the player who made the bid who announces an Alert.

LHO passed. Partner bid 2NT. RHO passed. How could I resist!

Dlr: East
Vul: Both

♠ AT865
♥ T95
♦ QT2
♣ A8

♠ 97
♥ J732
♦ J96
♣ J963

♠ K42
♥ 6
♦ AK843
♣ KQ52

♠ QJ3
♥ AKQ84
♦ 75
♣ T74

As soon as I tabled my cards, our opponents started yelling in Chinese at my partner, who could barely hide his smile as he raked in nine tricks. He had ducked the opening spade lead, won by East with the King. East then cashed the two top diamonds and continued the suit.

At the play of every card, the opponents took turns yelling at Shi. Being ever so polite to the foreign visitor, however, they took turns smiling at me, flashing enough teeth for any toothpaste commercial. Overlooked was the fact that they could have easily defeated 3NT with a club switch at trick two—or even at trick three.

Although I did not understand enough Chinese to know exactly what they were yelling about, I detected general statements about me and I knew they were not pleased with my 2 ♦ bid—that they considered it a psych, and psychs are not allowed in China, which is yet another story.

Was my bid a psych? Cuebids obviously have a different meaning in China—and they obviously still should be Alerted. Could no one in the cross-cultural, cross-linguistic, cross-gender conflict at my table discern that I had intended an international expression of the Western Cuebid?

At trick three, I reached over to the next table and grabbed the *Director* card out of the bidding box and waved it until two of them came over, examined the issue and instructed us to play on. Yes, I know I was dummy who is not supposed to call the Director, but things were getting out of hand.

The board was later thrown out and the women beat us 18-12 in Victory Points on the round. They came in fourth in the event. We were second.

If you had been my partner, how would you have explained the 2 ♦ bid to the opponents? And how would you have responded to their yelling at you while smiling at your partner?

CLASS A BRIDGE IN CHINA

Jilin Province is north of North Korea, and in October the weather is already showing signs of the Celsius-popping temperatures its winter is infamous for. I know, having spent the 1992 winter here. With a population of about two-and-a-half million, Changchun is its largest city, and also the site where the Japanese Unit 100 had conducted its chemical and biological experiments on live human subjects in the 1930s and 40s, now made famous by two episodes of *The X-Files*.

A three-hour flight from Hong Kong to Beijing and a tight connection before a two-hour flight to Changchun has brought me up here to play bridge with a friend and former partner Shi on the local Chess Academy team. The event is the annual Class A Provincial Championship, the first three teams automatically qualifying to go on to play in the National Championships in Beijing in December.

The event lasted a full week, with thirty seeded and twenty-four unseeded teams. The preliminary eighteen qualifying rounds narrowed the field down to sixteen teams. I am here for the finals, to slug it out over three days on the 30-point Victory Points scale. Because I had played for a year in Changchun before, and I have fewer than 10,000 masterpoints, special eligibility had to be extended to my participation in this event, with the clear understanding that since I am not a Chinese national, I would not qualify to go on with the team to the Beijing nationals, should we win.

The event was held at a downtown restaurant cleared for this event. Registration started early Friday morning, followed by a ceremony awarding consolation prizes to the teams that had been eliminated in the first four days of competition. The glad-handing provincial director of sports and recreation, who was clearly out of his element, handed out certificates embossed in three shades of red with attached gold tassels, along with his personal name card in English and Chinese, in three colors and listing all five of his administrative titles.

Since Shi and I had not played together in six years, we were trying to be both cautious and daring within the Walsh Two-over-One bidding system, struggling some with the timing and Lebensohl and responsive doubles at IMPs. The most exciting and at first disturbing feature of the match came from the kibitzers, and it appeared that all the players from the knocked-out thirty teams as well as their neighbors had stayed to watch the finals.

They would talk loudly to each other and comment on the bidding or card play as they moved around the tables. Occasionally I could hear what they were saying on my side of the diagonal curtain, feeling that they were destroying the intent of the bidding boxes and curtains. They walked from one side of the curtain to the other, looking at all four hands. And if it appeared that the hand was mundane and had no exciting potential, they would then walk to the next table and the next, in full view of the four directors and two scorers.

At one point I had to literally spank a hand that had reached across my shoulder to pick up the thirteen cards I had placed face down on the table. At the first break I asked our captain to complain to the head director, and as a consequence something was said over the loudspeaker at the beginning of the next match. But it didn't change the kibitzers' behavior—they've been told what not to do too many times in the past two centuries, by the Koreans, Russians, Japanese, Han Chinese, Mongolians, Germans, British, Americans, as well as Mao Tsetung, Chiang Kaishek, and the Red Guards, here in Jilin Province, formerly Manchukuo, that they defy authority whenever possible.

The Chess Academy team came in second, behind Jilin University. Most social and recreational events including bridge in this province are grouped around work units and officially recognized organizations. The teams that followed us in order were Jilin Oil Field, the 1st Automobile Factory (that manufactures Jeep Cherokees), Changchun Semiconductor Factory, the Auto Industry Higher Vocational School, and the Jilin Nickel Company.

Awards and on-going qualifying documents were passed out at the closing ceremonies, including good sportsmanship certificates. I collected my second place medal, but was disappointed that I would not be able to go on with the team to the Beijing Nationals.

REVENGE AT THE TABLE

After an adventurous and long train ride east from Chengdu that must have gone through at least one hundred tunnels and some of this planet's most spectacular countryside, I am in Kunming, in China's southwestern Yunnan Province. If one takes the trouble to think about what one is seeing on a journey away from the coast, the farther inland one travels and away from the guided tours, the more likely one will notice China's economic dark side that half a century of communist sovereignty has not eliminated.

Ah, Kunming, the high portal to the mythical Shangri-La imagined in James Hilton's *Lost Horizon*. Kunming, the over-the-Hump, Burma-to-China destination of the Flying Tigers in their P-40s and C-46ers, this century's first mercenaries, paid for by the U.S. in support of Old Peanut Head Generalissimo Chiang Kaishek's feeble attempts to ward off the Japanese incursion and occupation through most of the 1930s as well as World War II. Yunnan Province, at the head of the Golden Triangle made up of Burma, Laos, Vietnam and Thailand, which all serious drug trafficking had to go through for more than two centuries, and still does. It is rumored that one of Chiang Kaishek's army divisions, chasing Mao Tsetung's ragtag band of revolutionaries, abandoned its mission here and disappeared into the mountains to become wealthy drug traffickers. It was also here in Yunnan that Mao consolidated his followers in early 1934 and started his guerrilla retreat to the north and west.

Yunnan Province, here the local ethnic peoples outnumber the Han Chinese, and in fact vehemently do not consider themselves Chinese, which I discovered in a conversation with a local artist. But like their compatriots in Tibet and Mongolia and other marginal and occupied special regions and provinces in China, they are tightly ruled by the Han who have all the best-paying jobs and exercise an economic stranglehold on the province, while at the same time destroying the local culture by making it tourist curios.

On my second night I found a duplicate pairs game in a building next to the Number 3 Hospital, an ominous sign, I thought. Arriving a bit too late for a partner, I asked permission to kibitz behind the only woman player in the ten-table event with a non-playing director no older than twenty.

Reflecting the poorer economic situation of the region, the boards were made out of vinyl-covered cardboard which in regular club play could not last more than two years. There were also no bidding boxes as in Hong Kong, Beijing, Shanghai, or even Changchun, but players here wrote down their bids on a shared sheet of paper on which the board in play was placed.

In the hands that I watched, the overall quality of play was quite sound when compared to club games in the U.S. and elsewhere in China, except for one hand. I had chosen to kibitz the only woman player in the room because I have found that in China the women generally play better than men at most levels, and because this sister was clearly an ethnic minority because of her darker skin and simpler, less expensive clothing and didn't wear a watch, but mostly because in a room full of eager and anxious faces as if they've been in prison too long, she was relaxed and self-assured, not someone out to do a number. I will call her *Black Cat*.

Black Cat and her partner played the conventional Standard system with the nominal gadgets, as did all the other players at this game, excepting one pair clearly struggling with Precision. They were very gentle with each other, using eye contact rather than verbal communication when a *post mortem* was needed, especially after the hand which had a three trick swing from her table to the next.

As dealer and holding 18 HCPs with even distribution, Black Cat opened 1 NT holding ♠ A63 ♥ AJ75 ♦ AQ73 ♣ K8. Her partner checked for majors and placed the final contract at 3 NT.

                    ♠ KJ72
                    ♥ 832
                    ♦ T2
                    ♣ Q976
    ♠ 984   ♠ QT5
    ♥ T9   ♥ KQ64
    ♦ K965   ♦ J84
    ♣ A543   ♣ JT2
                    ♠ A63
                    ♥ AJ75
                    ♦ AQ73
                    ♣ K8

Black Cat blinked and looked across the table at her partner when his cards came down on the table in this ambitious contract. Looking at his cards, I thought down one at 3 NT for sure, even if she played double dummy, with a ♥ T opening lead. Playing his ♥ Q West split his honors, and Black Cat won with her ace. She next lost her ♠ J finesse to East's ♠ Q, who continued with the ♥ K and another ♥, his jaw dropping when West showed out of hearts, discarding a low ♦ for reasons known only to him.

Black Cat won with dummy's ♥ 8 and played an unsuccessful ♦ Q finesse. Winning with the ♦ K, East decided to turn loose a low ♠ to declarer's ♠ A. Black Cat cashed her winning ♥ J, with East discarding a ♣. Then a ♠ was led to dummy's ♠ K, and another ♠, arriving at this situation:

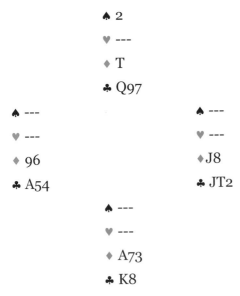

```
            ♠ 2
            ♥ ---
            ♦ T
            ♣ Q97
♠ ---                    ♠ ---
♥ ---                    ♥ ---
♦ 96                     ♦ J8
♣ A54                    ♣ JT2
            ♠ ---
            ♥ ---
            ♦ A73
            ♣ K8
```

On this last ♠ for a double squeeze, East decided to ditch a ♣, and Black Cat a ♦, and West threw in another ♦. A low ♣ came next, and East's ♣ T was covered by the ♣ K and taken by West's ♣ A before returning the ♦ 9, which really made no difference now, because Black Cat already has her nine tricks: three spades, three hearts, one diamond, and two clubs.

With an unexpected plus score of 600, Black Cat looked to her partner, a slight tinge of a smile in her eyes, as if saying that she had nothing to do with taking those nine tricks from the Han Chinese, who by now were looking out the window precipitously at the roof of the No. 2 Hospital next door. I had to bite my tongue to keep from getting up and leaving the table, but decided to stay and watch this same hand played at the next table where the bidding stopped at a sane but unimaginative 1 NT.

With a ♠ 9 out and a super defense, declarer winning only one ♥ trick, declarer went down one for a three-trick swing between these two consecutive tables! (After winning the ♠ A, declarer played a low ♥ from hand, with West winning with the ♥ 9 and continuing with the ♠ 8, which declarer won with dummy's ♠ K. Next came the ♥ 3, with East playing the ♥ 6, and declarer going up with the ♥ A and getting out with the ♥ 7. East won with the ♥ Q and played his ♣ J to dummy's ♣ Q, followed by a losing ♦ finesse. West rose to the occasion and dropped declarer's ♣ K with his ace, and exited with a ♣ to partner's ♣ T, who cased his remaining winners to set 1 NT one trick.)

It seems that while one may be politically, culturally, economically, sexually and spiritually oppressed away from the table, here in this game introduced by the colonizers, the odds are better, the field less sloped. In bidding and with luck in making the 3 NT contract, she exercised her revenge, at least symbolically, however its ephemeral meaning away from the table.

SHANGHAI SOLUTION

It was the week of January 26 and I was in Shanghai. In case I had forgotten that it was the Chinese New Year, the American Consulate General here made sure that I received a copy of William J. Clinton's New Year's greetings. The marvels of electronic mail prompted a reminder from a friend in Moscow, Idaho, that my celebration should include carrying lots of money (to bring wealth in the coming Year of the Tiger), keep my house (motel room?) clean (to have an orderly life) and to eat well (to promote good health).

A taxi took me to a club game, whizzing past several blocks of hyper-dense electronic communications and surveillance antennae belonging to the Maritime Customs Service, the only Chinese institution that has not been impacted by rampant corruption and stultifying bureaucracy in more than a century of its operation. The pre-arranged partnership included using the Precision system. Not having played Precision since the last time I used it in China in 1991, I should have been reviewing the opening 2 ♦ sequence and segregating it from the mini-Roman, Neapolitan and Acol's multicolored 2 ♦.

Instead, I was thinking about the cultural history of the Precision system. Yes, it's probably true the Chinese were the first to put together gunpowder. Yes, China has one of the oldest and quite possibly the longest recorded civilizations, however "Chinese" and "civilization" are defined. Yes, China (and not University of California-Berkeley?) produced one of the two greatest 20th century women physicists in Madame Chien Shiung Wu, and yes, it was a Chinese, C.C. Wei, who Terence Reese acknowledged had developed the Precision system more than anyone else. This form of cultural nationalism, or late xenophobia, can get a bit silly—not to mention boring and pointless, the same element that makes most summer Olympics broadcasts so unbearable.

On the second floor of an upscale shopping mall on the Bund, the playing site was spare and sparkled—two sections of tables with guide cards, bid boxes, plastic boards and scoresheets all neatly arranged a good half hour before game time. Unlike the younger directors in Hong Kong or Changchun, our director this day was in his 30s and clearly in charge—nobody was going to play late and not be penalized, no psych would go unrecorded, no nastiness would be tolerated at the table, and the final computerized score would be available no later than two minutes after the last traveler was turned in.

This was Shanghai, after all, and competitive bridge has been here for well over eighty years. Bridge had such a cultural presence here that the young boy in J.G. Ballard's *Empire of the Sun,* set in Shanghai during World War II, "after years spent listening to his mother's bridge parties, trying to extract any kind of logic from the calls of 'One Diamond,' 'Pass,' 'Three Hearts,' 'Three No Trumps,' 'Double,' 'Redouble,' [embarked] on the most difficult chapter of all, on psychic bidding—all this and he had yet to play a single hand..."

As I looked over the standings which were, indeed, posted within two minutes after the last score was turned in, I was asked by the director to serve on a seven-member appeals committee over a deal that we defended at 3NT, making for a below average score.

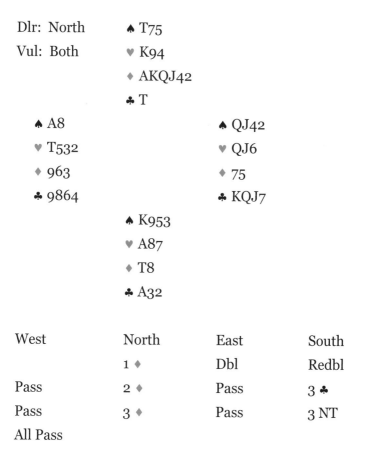

Dlr: North	♠ T75
Vul: Both	♥ K94
	♦ AKQJ42
	♣ T

♠ A8		♠ QJ42
♥ T532		♥ QJ6
♦ 963		♦ 75
♣ 9864		♣ KQJ7

| ♠ K953 |
| ♥ A87 |
| ♦ T8 |
| ♣ A32 |

West	North	East	South
	1 ♦	Dbl	Redbl
Pass	2 ♦	Pass	3 ♣
Pass	3 ♦	Pass	3 NT
All Pass			

The director had been called to this table by East after North had held a Pass card for a few seconds before returning it to the bid box. The director ruled that the Pass had not been "established" and allowed North to replace it with 2 ♦, and when the deal was over he ruled that 3 NT by South making would stand. The director ruled that South had not used information he may have gained from North's handling of his Pass card, hence Law 16A governing unauthorized information did not apply.

The committee voted 5—2 in favor of upholding the director's ruling. The committee believed that an infraction had occurred, but five of us agreed with the director that no extraneous information had been transmitted and that South's 3 NT was logical considering his hand.

The two who voted against the majority argued that the director had made a mistake in his ruling, that he should have applied Law 25 (change of call), in which case his partner (South) would not have had another call. We voted this way even though we realized that our argument was inapplicable, since that had not been the contention of the appeal.

This was the week of the new Year of the Tiger, in which everyone is focused on celebrating wealth, order and health, so the committee unanimously added a second decision to avoid any acrimony, one provided by Law 82. We awarded East-West an adjusted score of average without penalizing North-South, and keeping the committee meeting in less than fifteen Shanghai-efficient minutes.

THE DAY THE WAR ENDED IN SHANGHAI

I was six the day the war ended in 1945
But I don't remember which flag I waved

There were carnivals everywhere
The regulators were beginning to disappear

The radio station sent out free news
Prison doors opened for fifty today, one hundred tomorrow

One by one they came out, the Red Cross relocating
The head in one place, the feet in another

Most said nothing, others still stood in line
Promising to vote "A" or "A" in the next election

*

There I am, in that photograph trying to look away
The day the war ended on this street corner

Those others gathered around me were waiting
Blowing out kisses to *Movietone News*

They lingered, trying to believe whatever happened
Will not be repeated in another history

*

Now at more than a half century since that war ended
Our stories are still hedged between hurt and hope

Most of the time I'm watching eyewitness news
As if I'm seeing something taking place in the past

Or between there and here, whatever the time
These intolerances have not stopped, whatever the place

This is what it was like exactly that day after
With nothing left to be taken away

Someone is tracing a distant coincidence
Another is doing the same in his head

We are all waiting for messages or decisions
Our fists gripped in ambiguity, between wars

BEIJING DISSIDENTS AT THE WASHINGTON MALL

This man Wang is serious. He has put a map of the Mall in Liu's hands and is insisting that after meeting with the media at the Washington Monument, the parade/demonstration must be routed to the White House for a final statement.

You're crazy, Liu shouted above the other voices, a strategy he had learned at Columbia's democracy salon. "We'll need two permits. One from the Park Service for the Mall maybe, but the city will never give us one for Pennsylvania Avenue on the same day. No way. Impossible."

Wang shook his sheen of shoulder-length hair from side to side, practicing for the TV cameras. It glistened in the subdued light of the living room. It's gorgeous, and its image has already been beamed to every TV set on both sides of the Pacific. Then abruptly he looked straight at Liu, his seriousness and sincerity focused for the photojournalist's close-up.

Look, we're all here. Wang swept his arm around the crowded apartment. Even double-exiled Black Dog from San Diego.

We know, we know, yelled someone from the kitchen. Where he's been selling Yamaha guitars after his expulsion from Berkeley for lying about his green card. *YA-MA-HA.* Ha, ha, ha. Good thing he lives in California. For penance now he must bring his Nanjing grandmother oranges every morning for breakfast.

We must be serious here, Wang continued. Wang the career organizer, who has put this curious coalition together. COC, he called us, Committee of Overseas Chinese, ever watchful of human rights violations in China and always promoting the struggle for democracy in the motherland.

But what he said was true, we're all here, half of Beijing's leaders' children all gathered in one room in America's capital, the third brain drain this century—Qing from Brandeis who still slept with the lights on, Gao holding down a Nieman at Harvard, Liu from CUNY, and even Crazy Li from Michigan State. A casually tossed grenade here would seriously alter China's future on both sides of the Pacific.

We must also select someone to make the speech, that same voice yelled from the kitchen.

What about the physicist Fang Lizhi? Xiao Liu raised her hand. She was rumored to be dating an American, but she has not yet changed her Beijing-styled bobbed hair or cotton shoes.

No, that won't work, Wang answered. Nobody trusts a physicist, not anymore, not since Galileo.

He wasn't a physicist, you idiot, Black Dog shuddered. But I agree with you. Fang's not very good in front of a camera, in either language, Chinese or English, physics or politics.

The silence of agreement, the vast stillness of conspiracy hatched some ten years ago in Beijing, before the first gathering in front of the Gate of Heavenly Peace in April, 1989.

We need someone younger, someone with good teeth, someone who'll make those mothers in Peoria and Schenectady cry over their TV dinners and send us their checks before their husbands come home, Xiao Liu volunteered. Ever the consensus builder, she had not yet abandoned her role of saying what everyone else in the room was already thinking.

All right then, what about Wang Dan? Someone had to say it, and it was Black Dog. He's recognizable, even for America's short memory. Good in front of cameras, and he sounds convincing with his new dentures. He even mentions those prisoners that have been left behind—surely that will wring more hearts for our cause.

Yeah, but there's always that rogue reporter out there who's going to make him slip, even with an interpreter. It happened twice last year, in Milwaukee and in Denver. Wang sounded very sure of himself—he had stopped shaking his hair for that announcement. He's going to be our next president; we can't expose him to any negative publicity so early.

What about that student who stopped the tanks during the demonstration at Tiananmen Square? asks Simon Fraser's Chen, a wannabe from the south who speaks a passable Mandarin but has been accepted because of his success at raising funds from Hong Kong's motherland candle burners.

You mean Charlie Cole's *Newsweek* photo that's been reprinted all over the world a million times every June 4 since 1989? Black Dog asked between sucks on his funky cigarette. I thought everyone knew he didn't stop those tanks of the 38th Army in T-Square; those four unarmed tanks stopped for him. It isn't just a squabble between interpretations. I thought everyone knew that. Strange that we've never been able to identify him. Perhaps he was a MSS agent?

Or he was a student swiftly arrested and imprisoned, Chen argued.

All right, you two, all right, Wang interceded, shaking his hair. Let's not fight among ourselves. We still have a lot to decide before meeting with the Park Service tomorrow.

Hey, let's order out some Chinese, that same person yelled from the kitchen. That'll get some work done.

*　*　*

The next morning Wang, Black Dog, Xiao Liu and Liu were at the Park Service office filling out a form for a parade/demonstration permit. We had been there for more than an hour, and were having some problems with the questions of our organization's address and list of officers.

Looks like you could do with some friendly assistance with that form, a woman's voice drifted from the blind side. A ranger with shorter hair than Xiao Liu's had come to help.

Yes. Thanks, ma'am, Wang said and turned around, shaking his hair.

Please don't *ma'am* me, the ranger said. I'm here to help, and my name is Dorene Okamura, she smiled, patting her burnished nameplate over her left pocket.

Wang looked at Liu, who pretended not to know what the look meant. Instead Liu handed Dorene Okamura the form and the Park Service ballpoint pen.

This is as far as we've come, Liu explained.

The Washington Monument, that's okay. Fifteenth and Constitution, still within the Mall, Dorene Okamura read the form. Let's see here. Okay so far. Hmmm.

Xiao Liu was beaming with admiration.

October 10. Hmmm. That might be a problem, Dorene Okamura looked at me. Another group has also applied for a permit for the same time that day. Perhaps you? Human Rights Watch, Human Rights in China, and AI?

We didn't know. It was Wang who answered.

Ranger Okamura continued to talk to Liu, as if his running shoes, baseball hat, and no cloud of tobacco stink encircling him made him less likely to misunderstand her words.

But we can work it out, she said. They'll be going up Constitution Avenue. Would you have any problems if the two groups saw each other from a distance of four blocks?

She was directing the question to Liu again, but it is Wang who answered, again.

No problem, he said, in the same tone of voice as if the ranger had just changed her order from a Big Mac to a double cheeseburger. Who's their speaker, he added.

I think Were Kaiser, but I'm not sure.

Yes, you mean Wu'er Kaixi, that Uighur minority hooligan from Beijing Normal, that exploiter of human tragedy? I thought he was in Australia somewhere or Japan, last I heard.

Wherever, Dorene Okamura said. But they said he'll be here October 10. 10:45 a.m. The media's been notified. My job is to see to three things: first that there'll be no conflict between the two parades; then ensure the media will have appropriate access to both groups in an orderly manner; and make sure there will be enough Porta Potties for everyone. We also provide the necessary deputized security to make sure these things will happen, and in the right order, and first aid, if necessary.

Liu could see that Xiao Liu wanted to know what a Porta Potti was, but she looked down at the floor tiling instead, suppressing the question for later.

These demonstration requirements look pretty controlled and rehearsed to me, Black Dog spoke for the first time. Whatever happened to good old spontaneous demonstration?

We happen to believe there's never been a spontaneous demonstration in human history. Ranger Okamura looked ready for the cameras. Not even in front of the Hilton in 1968 Chicago. In Indonesia last year, first a truck shows up with the demonstrators, then a minute later another truck loaded with rocks. They are all planned, some more successfully than others.

If any of your people plan on being at high places, she added, such as rooftops, monuments, or trees, we must know where and their names.

The four of us took turns looking at each other and said nothing.

The ranger continued.

There'll be a staging area available to you at nine. She talked to the wall map and pointed to a small section off the freeway at the junction of Independence and Third. Here you can organize your pro-democracy parade. Are you sure you don't know about the other group? She looked straight at Wang, who was busily shaking his hair, which has become his answer to everything he wanted to avoid.

Black Dog and Liu exchanged looks to say nothing, and it is Xiao Liu who answered the ranger.

Yes, at the staging area we can put on makeup for the cameras. Some powder so our faces won't shine under the bright lights. Some lipstick, too. We must look young, energetic, and dedicated to democracy.

The rest of the details were worked out quickly with the efficient ranger, before the four of them drove over to the Georgetown Mall to look for just the right shade of Revlon, maybe a *Cappuccino* or *Natural Nude,* so they won't kiss off, so they would continue to believe.

(Many of the student activists at the 1989 Tiananmen Square demonstration were children of some of the very top political leaders in China, who were welcomed by some of the leading American educational institutions. Several "pro-democracy" rallies were held in this country to raise funding for its movement, and this narrative was provided by one of these dissidents, whose name has been changed.)

Section 3

Post Colonial Hong Kong

HONG KONG AS CASH COW

The Overseas Chinese came into existence as a direct consequence of China's first unification under the Qin Dynasty some 2,000 years ago. Such a massive, dynastic undertaking exacerbated existing feuds and alliances, in the process creating new political and economic identities. Some of the bodies of these new political enemies were absorbed into the Great Wall and other monster civil construction projects as prisoner-laborers, some changed their identities and went underground, and the rest were dumped as illegal aliens south of the Yangtze River into *yueh,* a wilderness peopled by rice eaters. Such a political morphology indicates that sometimes China is better understood as a geographic and political entity with approximate, blurring and sometimes conflicting or opaque boundaries, rather than as a *nation* in the nineteenth and twentieth century sense. However China is perceived as a political entity, what is clear is that in the past centuries these Overseas Chinese have become the economic engine of much of Asia, in the process relocating successively to the south, so that today the term *Offshore Chinese* more accurately describes their geographic and economic personae.

At 55 million today, this Offshore Chinese empire comprises only 4 percent of China's total population, but its GNP of US$450 billion is higher than China's, and its current liquid capital is estimated by a Singapore banker at as much as US$2 trillion. Much of this capital has been accumulated since the end of World War II and its aftermath, when Western investments were either pulled out or kicked out of Asia. The Offshore Chinese were well-positioned geographically to be the recipients of orphaned property and flight capital, their organization, network and hard-driving work ethic earning the benefits of the convulsive ownership changes during the decolonization of much of East and South Asia.

Such indications that the Chinese have been more successful in their diaspora communities have meant that on some very significant level their southern and offshore accumulation of wealth as power has been their ultimate revenge upon the north's exercise of sometimes tyrannical political power. Beijing may be the political capital of the kingdom, but Hong Kong will be its economic capital, roughly the difference between New York and Washington. Such a distinction has not been lost on Beijing, whose handpicked members assigned to draft the *Basic Law* document under which the Hong Kong Special Administrative Region will exist favored the conservative business side. It also meant the creation of an entire late capitalistic merchant middle class topped by a small but super-powerful elite with no flag, government or allegiances. These Offshore Chinese hold multiple residencies in such cities as Taipei, Singapore, Los Angeles, Bangkok, Jakarta, Hong Kong and now Vancouver, and their family members carry passports from multiple nations and fly first class in Boeing 747s.

Some argue that the main wave of the entrepreneurial Offshore Chinese immigrated to Hong Kong about the time Chairman Mao declared the success of the communist revolution atop Beijing's Tiananmen Square in October of 1949, others that this most recent exodus from Shanghai only augmented what has always been a merchant-conscious, multi-national community in a natural port that boasts no other natural resources. In whatever perspective the origins are interpreted, it is clear that in the past half-century, Hong Kong has become, in the words of its last governor Christopher Patten, a vibrant, efficient, hard-working community under a British administration dedicated to free-market economics.

This has meant that some of these Offshore Chinese in Hong Kong can park investments in local housing and land developments as well as in shopping centers in the United States. Others play the gold market, commodities and futures. Still others buy start-up software development companies. All these transactions are legal, sometimes masked and shielded behind countless intermediaries.

During this period, such transnational entrepreneurial successes have shamed the Hong Kong Jockey Club dropping its racist barrier to membership, and had an impact on the social, economic and political demographics of this Crown Colony. It is also reflected in China's recognition of the strategic importance of the burgeoning economic powerhouse that it has left Hong Kong alone, even in its nastiest confrontations with Taiwan, the U.S. and the U.K. It is no coincidence that three

Special Economic Zones encircle Hong Kong geographically, and that China's helmsman Deng Xiaoping made his "to-be-rich-is-glorious," "Step More Boldly into Capitalism" speech in Shenzhen, a city sharing a border with Hong Kong.

In many ways Hong Kong is a cash cow. It is a cash cow to everybody, from the Offshore Chinese to the British rulers, but also for the people who just happen to stop by looking for a job to the Chinese companies and industries hundreds of miles from Hong Kong. With the digital clock in Beijing's Tiananmen Square ticking off the hours before Hong Kong's return to China at midnight on June 30, 1997, there has been a rush of applicants from Liverpool, London, and Birmingham trying to beat the April 1 cutoff deadline for Britishers applying for guaranteed work permits.

Such entrepreneurial spirit has meant that conglomerates involving property, aviation, telecommunications and civil works (when completed, the new Hong Kong airport will be the world's largest engineering project) have found it necessary to reinvest its accumulated capital back in China. It is estimated that more than sixty percent of foreign investments in China can be traced to the Offshore Chinese in Hong Kong, and that close to forty percent of China's export trade is conducted through Hong Kong as the world's largest container port. During this transitional period, other nations have tried to get their hands on this Offshore Chinese capital by selling legal residencies pending citizenship, under the label of *Investment Immigrant*—currently Canada charges US$300,000, the U.S. US$1,000,000, but several south American countries are satisfied with a lot less.

Additionally, what started in the 1950s as small mom-and-pop industries such as toy manufacturing, garment industries, and some patent-defying enterprises, has shifted inland into the lower-waged Special Economic Zones next to Hong Kong, in turn making them the economic envy of the rest of China. In return, during the various periods of buying opportunities such as the 1982 Hang Seng Index decline in reaction to the UK's acknowledgement of China's claim to Hong Kong, China has more than US$20 billion invested in Hong Kong, and will soon replace the United Kingdom as the largest owner of the market. This mutually beneficial relationship is perhaps best illustrated in the intricate 1996 financial transactions between China's CITIC Pacific and the British Swire Pacific that resulted in CITIC purchasing twenty-five percent of Hong Kong's airline company. Another scenario involves the Carrian Group which in the late 1970s bought huge nuggets of Kowloon's Golden Mile on Nathan Road and the Gammon House block in downtown Hong Kong in addition to real estate investments in California and Florida and significant controlling shares of China Underwriters Life and Union Bank. The 1992 Carrian Group bankruptcy mirrored the Hang Seng Index dramatic slump in response to the British-Chinese negotiations over Hong Kong futures.

While the World Bank was mucking about with low-risk, long-range and sometimes low-yield investments in a shrimp patch here, yet another questionable dam on some Third World river there, the Offshore Chinese have been making high-risk and high-return and short-turnaround investments, most of the time landing on their feet. World Bank analysts have predicted that China will be the world's major economic power by 2010.

The editors of *The Economist* have joined in such anticipation by describing China's economic boom as "the most significant development since the industrial revolution," and the president of Templeton Emerging Markets Fund has predicted that Hong Kong's Hang Seng Index will hit 20,000 before the end of 1997.

There has been much speculation in the Western press in the last year about what will happen to Hong Kong after the June 30/July 1 handover. The closer we are, the more shrill and irrelevant the commentaries become. Some discussion has focused on what will happen to the freest press in the world, which it is not. In a tabloid format, the Hong Kong press has enjoyed a long reputation of being free to focus on the most pressing gossip and the most benign political and economic issues, because speculation was the only game in town. In many significant ways, it has been a colonized press. During some of the early 1950s demonstrations, residents caught reading a copy of any alternative newspaper were arrested and detained for political questioning, and an ordinance was passed in 1951 prohibiting the publication of any *subversive* material and granting the government stop-and-seize powers.

During his recent visit to China, the U.S. House Speaker Newt Gingrich displayed the legacy of former Secretary of State John Foster Dulles' Bamboo Curtain rhetoric by describing Hong Kong's return to China as a gorilla holding an orchid. Ignoring the known intention of this metaphor, one might ask who is the gorilla and who the orchid in this complex political and economic scenario.

On another level, in the U.S. media the description of Deng Xiaoping was always accompanied by the epithet that he was short, containing the view that racially we know who is in power here, the tall ones from the West. From the inaccurate and often distorted information published in the media, the average American is opposed to any expenditure of American dollars that would fill the coffers of China's People's Liberation Army bent on invading the United States, a throwback to the nineteenth century European and American construction of the Chinese peoples as The Yellow Peril, justifying imperialism for conquest and control. Leslie Stahl's April 6 CBS *Sixty Minutes*' piece on Hong Kong showed how she not only completely missed the point in her coverage of the changeover, but that she was ideologically duplicitous in her sympathetic interview with Governor Patten and her adversarial interview with the Beijing-designated next leader, Tung Chee-hwa. Fearful of increasing the third-largest immigrant group of 100,000 Chinese, the United Kingdom fared no better in passing a new British Nationality Law which decreed that Hong Kongers holding this kind of passport would have no right to reside in the UK.

Much of the subtext of this kind of reaction is racist, that we are not discussing nationality, economic, political or ideological issues, but that they are racialist masks for the fact that China is about the only nation in the world that has escaped European imperialism, the passage of Hong Kong into British hands in 1841 being a dangerously close call. Western hegemony demands that the *Mongolian horde* rhetoric of the nineteenth century be revived and translated into photographic exhibitions of the People's Liberation Army posing a new *oriental* threat.

And finally, such innate responses are simplified into one intellectually justifiable issue: China does not respect human rights. Fortunately U.S. Secretary of State Madeleine Albright sees the necessity of de-linking the human rights issue from political and economic relations with China, and that foreign policy should not be held hostage by any one issue.

For the Offshore Chinese in Hong Kong, the real issue after the changeover at the end of this month is not whether the one-country two-systems would work. If the transition fails and the two-systems collapses, it is Beijing that will have more to lose. The Hong Kongers would simply withdraw their sheltered and protected investments and move offshore one more time where their talent, education (presently one in four in Hong Kong has a college education), industry and venture capital will be welcomed anywhere where race is not a factor. Under these circumstances, the recently constructed nostalgic patriotic view of China as Motherland will diminish as these ever-pragmatic Offshore Chinese seize new opportunities and form new alliances.

The real issue is how fast China's political reform will catch up with the nation's meteoritic economic growth and how much autonomy Hong Kong can maintain as the contractual broker between the rest of China and the rest of the world. As the former President of the Soviet Union Mikhail Gorbachev has recently said about China, "In the final analysis, I think one cannot democratize the economy while leaving all the rest as it was before. Even within a one-party system, greater pluralism is necessary." As for China, he said that they will do it "in their own way. We have to hope for the best from this process. All of us have a stake in the stability of the huge world called China."

Perhaps another significant issue rests inside the proposal of the one-system, two countries, in which Hong Kong upon the failure of the present political infrastructure will lead the Special Economic Zones which surround it in a break-away from Beijing and form yet a third China with Hong Kong as its capital. This discussion would certainly deserve more merit than such speculations as How free the press will be in Hong Kong, Will Hong Kong be China's colony, How much will dissent be tolerated, Will the fledgling labor unions be allowed to exist, Will Hong Kong be adopted into China's postal numerical system, Will the judiciary be able to maintain its independence under the new Basic Law, How representative will the elections be, Will the Hong Kong system be really allowed to continue uninterrupted and unfettered for the next fifty years as promised in the 1984 Joint Declaration, and Will all residents be forced to use chopsticks.

It is interesting to note that these questions and issues have been surfacing with alarming frequency as the calendar approaches June 20, even though most of their realities have existed unchallenged for the last one-hundred and fifty-six years under British rule. It is no secret that given the opportunity, including education at a *home* college or military academy, the colonized often surpass their masters in their ability to mimic and reproduce the imperial hegemony.

For the Offshore Chinese, whatever happens to the economic future of Hong Kong, the goose will still lay golden eggs under a different diet. Nothing new. It's happened before.

A slight change of offshore geography could also mean that from their new locations they will become more active players in the developing global gentrification created by late capitalism's latest expression.

(This essay was written a year before Hong Kong's return to China in 1997, and before Shanghai regained its former prominent economic position.)

THE RE-TAKING OF HONG KONG

There has been much speculation about the political, economic and cultural consequences of Hong Kong's reunification with China on July 1, 1997. The creation of a Special Administrative Region has positioned the former British Crown colony of 155 years at the tail end of the *One-Country, Two-Systems* political paradigm, with China's promise that Hong Kong will be free to determine its own domestic future, including the freedom to practice a form of democracy that was inconceivable under British rule. Hyphenations are not new to Hong Kong; its placement in this handover's double hyphen, however, introduces new elements into an already complex and labyrinthine case history that defies existing modes of cultural interpretation. What emerges as the only unarguably clear conclusion in this re-photographic exploration of Hong Kong's public space sited almost half a century apart, is a unique form of late capitalism in which everything exists just at the point of disappearance.

To be expected in this political handover, Queen Elizabeth II's portrait has disappeared from Hong Kong's public domain, postage stamps and currency, as well as such epithets as *Royal* and *H.M.S.* from uniforms and letterheads. At the nation-state level, the Union Jack has been replaced by the silhouette of a pea blossom against a red background flown at public sites to the left of the Chinese flag, and reappears on stamps and currency, as well as public trash bins, gift calendars and coffee mugs made in China.

Hong Kongers are not Chinese, as if China or any other country could be meaningfully defined in such general terms, whatever the period. Hong Kongers stopped being Chinese the moment they left their mainland villages or cities whenever. In coming to Hong Kong, much of their previous identities were surrendered along with their passports to the Immigration Department at the border crossing, and what has emerged in the transplantation are new cultural formations: fragments of the old; hybrids with the new; and hyphenations with whoever else expats that separate as well as connect.

This has included language for most, whose other Chinese dialects had disappeared, replaced by the indigenous Hong Kong Cantonese. This has also included the creation of new customs that are alleged to have been inherited from their parents, their unassailable claim to being Chinese: for instance, to ward off bad luck, one never buys a car on a Buddhist holiday; one never accepts a credit card or bank account number divisible by four; and one never kills a spider on one's birthday. Their origins have been forgotten, so it is said, but their disappearance that places these traditions outside the bounds of historical scrutiny thereby makes their otherwise unexplainable practice that much more profound, especially to the unsuspecting tourist mistaking *kitsch* for the authentic.

As a colonized Asian people, Hong Kongers have been assigned to live in the mythical and oppressive world as represented by *The World of Suzie Wong* and *Love Is a Many Splendored Thing*, and such functioning but distorted perceptions that Hong Kong is where *East Meets West,* the *Pearl of the Orient* nicknamed *Fragrant Harbour,* and that Hong Kong is bi-lingual. For the natives, negotiating this kind of cultural schizophrenia has necessitated the donning of two masks, one in the front, and one in the back. Indeed, Hong Kong's pea blossom icon that has been identified on the global level as an orchid (see Speaker of the House Newt Gingrich's perception of the relationship between China and Hong Kong as a gorilla holding an orchid in its hand) is not an orchid at all, but more correctly a pea tree, *Bauhinia blakeana Dunn* (*Caesalpiniaceae*), not a natural species, but appropriately for Hong Kong, a sterile, hothouse hybrid named after a former governor.

The disappearance of the British icons and their instantaneous substitutions are not new to Hong Kong. Hong Kongers have always worn two faces simultaneously, one in public for the public, and the other also public but one waiting for the next public: on one level, one is presented to the British colonizers and their various representations, and the other to relatives and proven friends. During the Korean War and much of the 1950s Cold War, for example, the necessity for the public-public face almost spelled the demise of the next-public face, as the Chinese and Kuomintang sent down competing assassination squads in an attempt to reverse the brain drain. The British rulers refereed from the sidelines to minimize the drain on Hong Kong's bloodbank and maintain local stability by arresting and detaining just about every known political activist without trial, sometimes on the whimsical evidence of reading the wrong newspaper in public.

Even the way they drive in the Hong Kong streets and few miles of highways, and the manner they walk in its numerous crowded shopping malls and streets, reflect their awareness of a disappearing public space, in the same way that colonized peoples all over the world have learned to hide behind anonymity. The drivers have disappeared behind the smoked glass of their late model cars, their automated personae ruthlessly slipping the car into any empty space available, lest some other car—not its driver—occupy it first. This contested public space is viewed impersonally as something that must be taken before it too disappears, or before it is grabbed up by someone else. Walking in public space also articulates personal greed at the intersection of personal place and public space!

Hyperdensity in Hong Kong is not caused by limited space alone. It is also exacerbated by economic greed and government duplicity in subsidizing big business at investing not only in property development, but the associated retention and reproduction of cheap labor and guaranteed minimal salary demands. When Hong Kong's new airport opens in April on Lantau Island, the height restriction on Kowloon's highrises in the way of the present airport's only flight path will be raised, providing yet another investment opportunity for both the government as well as private speculators. The existing buildings will disappear and be replaced by even higher multi-storied apartments at above $2,000 per square foot.

It was in this economically driven context in 1953 that the Chinese government opened its Bank of China office as one of Hong Kong's first highrises, the fourteen-storied building at No. 2 Des Voeux Road, pictured below, lower center. The U.S. Seventh Fleet with its dominating fast pitch softball teams can also be seen in the middle of Victoria Harbour as an aircraft carrier and several attending destroyers and supply vessels.

This *old* Bank of China building is overshadowed by skyscrapers in the following image, re-taken almost forty-four years later of the same site from the exact same spot with essentially the same photographic equipment, 2¼ Rolleiflex. U.S. warships have not entered the harbor in years, since parts of the harbor have also disappeared from the massive reclamation projects that have forced the newer, larger warships to anchor in deeper waters next to outlying Lantau Island, such as the *USS Nimitz* in September of this year.

Such instant displacements have made Hong Kong's landscape unrecognizable for anyone who has been away for more than a year. Such disappearances and cover-overs would be normally expected of a minimally-regulated, capital-intense, commerce-driven profit economy. Commercial and residential buildings go up and down with such regularity that meaningful concepts of individual and community identities must be flexible and adaptive, if not altogether non-existent. When the Ritz-Carlton Hotel was near its completion in 1993, the original owners disappeared after selling it to a multinational consortium that seriously considered savaging the luxury hotel before a single guest had registered, and resurrecting in its place an office highrise because of the potential higher profit. Today in 1997, this hotel has been totally renovated into luxury apartment units; the hotel disappeared after only three years of tourist service.

The remarkable *new* Bank of China building completed in May 1990 at No. 1 Garden Road, and seen from a few eastern-facing windows of the *newest* version of the Ritz-Carlton, is a 70-storied skyscraper visible from most of Kowloon across the harbor, and the higher elevations of the harbor side of Hong Kong, constructed or natural. Looking at it from the Peak—formerly named *Victoria* [again] *Peak*—in the lower right of the image, this diagonally-themed power tower was designed by the distinguished American architect I.M. Pei. Along with the highrises too many to count, it has totally obliterated the constructed features in its twin image taken half a century ago on the previous page. That the *old* Bank of China building is one of the few that have survived this period between their two exposures attests to a precarious permanency attributable to its numerology as No. 2, and the hope that Pei's *new* Bank of China building occupying No. 1 would survive most of the 21st century, even in the Hong Kong clock of bigger-better-higher-more-expensive commodification.

Commodity by definition is mass production in all of its variants and limitations. Its product usually has a short life, is eliminated, thrown away, laid waste, and then just as quickly resurrected, re-marketed and re-consumed in endless cycles. It has often been said that Hong Kong re-invents itself every few years, and that the disappearance of the old must be a prerequisite for the emergence of the new. A quick look at Kowloon's Austin Road's new (last year) apartment buildings next to the old (ten years) standing side-by-side shows a rare moment, rare in the sense that signs of age and decay are visible, since buildings are obliterated and made to disappear before they have had a chance to become old.

In the economics of this changing cycle of the new replacing the old, how more appropriate that the old colonial domestics who immigrated to Hong Kong historically from neighboring Guangdong Province as house servants and nannies have been replaced in the last decade by Filipino women at next-to-the-lowest racist rung. Like their Guangdong predecessors whose choices in life were severely restricted to the service trades, these 200,000 *amahs* take on an identity that confronts and frustrates their masters—many of whom were *amahs* a generation ago—at least on Sundays on holidays.

Sure they still do the shopping, cooking, laundry, ironing, cleaning, garbage disposal and are certified in CPR, and they still walk the dogs and take care of the children. But on Sundays and public holidays they dramatically defy disappearance.

Congregated in small groups along some of the world's most expensive sidewalks, in front of the Hang Seng Bank, the five-starred Mandarin Oriental Hotel or a similar billion-dollar building, they are not out-of-sight and not out-of-mind. These all-day picnic gatherings include mats for their food, drink, song and games. Their territoriality based on shared dialect and geographic origin can identify them as that group from Luzon, that one from Manila, and that from Baguio, a virtual map of the Philippines. They are also the vulnerable sheep to American evangelicals, including the Church of the Latter Day Saints, the Southern Baptist Convention, the Missouri Synod Lutherans, and especially the Pentecostals. What an ironic public statement against this newest variation of late-capitalism that is Hong Kong, this gargantuan economic imbalance in which a very few are making fortunes from other people's misery.

Currently there is a growing billion-dollar industry that focuses on historical preservation, and it is linked to Hong Kong's attempt to re-take its identity by turning to its past, by looking at its landmark buildings, by looking at old sepia photographs from which to construct a visual narrative of its own history, to not be a colonized people in their own country, whatever the number of hyphens. It is interesting to note that this effort had its beginnings only after Prime Minister Margaret Thatcher and Premier Zhao Ziyang signed the Sino-British Joint Declaration in Beijing in 1984 that signaled the return of Hong Kong to China.

Such preservation inherent in the construction of public memory plays a crucial role in the restoration of place and hence history, however facile and however inaccurate, particularly in the hands of the post-colonialists. They are more interested in investing in the artifacts such as authentic native furniture, paintings, even costumes, than they are in the total human experience including the pain and suffering that sometimes accumulate in shit. Their interest in preservation stems in part in their effort to alleviate their guilt, in part as re-colonization in the act of cultural piracy, except that now they have to cash up, and in part as an honest attempt to see what they've ignored for nearly two hundred years. The restoration of Kowloon's Walled City devoid of its drugs, prostitution, and other forms of human misery, has elevated it into the most sophisticated expression of *kitsch*, the theme park for tourists.

If the military is the first outpost of imperialism, then surely culture will be short-listed as its last. But, not before the natives have acquired the practice of mimicking the masters, sometimes surpassing the rulers in this corollary to their masters attempting to preserve local culture. This is not a secret in the power exchange between rulers and natives. Look at Vietnam in the 1950s and 1960s for a recent example. In the continuing saga of periodic re-invention, Hong Kong's recent reunification might even be regarded as an opportunity for another makeover. The expatriates have all but disappeared from the formerly racially segregated Hong Kong Jockey Club, its car park currently occupied by the latest Mercedes, Jaguars, BMWs, Rolls-Royces and Ferraris owned by the Hong Kong-Chinese new rich who are definitely into symbols of conspicuous consumption to the extreme. Expensive watches that begin at $10,000, pens at $1,000 and jewelry are displayed prominently on a more portable level. A Provisional Legislator has built a replica Bordeaux wine cellar into his office suite with temperature and humidity controls, two air conditioners guaranteeing a constant

16° C environment behind thermal glass panes so that visitors can see through them—a dramatic display for someone who freely admits that he doesn't even like wine. Another spent $54,000 on wine at a dinner for six, so that—as he proudly admitted in an interview—he could be noticed.

Perhaps this dramatic, symbolic flaunting of economic excess is a statement about the need for claiming a personal narrative, a stay against a vanishing background. For now, against this changing landscape of the last half a century, there remains one inexpensive, nostalgic constant that has not disappeared: the green-and-white reliable Star Ferry that connects Kowloon and Hong Kong every twenty minutes, at 30 cents a crossing in first class. Count them: Day Star, Solar Star, Morning Star, Northern Star, World Star, Shining Star, Night Star, Golden Star, Celestial Star, Silver Star, Meridian Star, and of course, Twinkling Star. Take a ride now—who knows how soon the ongoing reclamation projects will make even the harbor disappear.

(October, 1997)
(A late update. Connie Bragas-Regaldo, chair of United Filipinos in Hong Kong, was upset on February 3, 1998, when the government, anticipating a temporary economic downturn, announced a freeze on the minimum monthly wage at US$498.26 for foreign domestic workers. She argued that her constituents would be equally impacted by the economic forecast, if not more so.)

LATERAL VIOLENCE

200,000 foreign domestic helpers (Hong Kong
Departments of Labour & Immigration, 1997)

*Decolonization is quite simply the replacing a certain
species by another species, an absolute substitution.*
– Franz Fanon, *The Wretched of the Earth*

They curse the exact work done a generation
Ago by those lucky enough to have made
The border crossing just in time to become
Today's arrogance. Entrusted to keep homes

And lives clean, they are despised—*Dir-ty!*
Do-mes-tic! Ah-mah!—like their employers were
Who now spit them out as only the Cantonese
Still determined to find their mother tongue

For vengeance can. Come on in at any floor
Jump out any other in this vertical novel
That is Hong Kong, on any day stained
Chrome and glass if you want. There are

More than 200,000 of them here, mostly
Women, mostly Filipinas, this Maria.
By calling them member of the family
They are contracted into accepting endless

And ever-changing lists, duties, timetables
Special rules, *Don't use the telephone*
So expatriate wives are released to shop
Lunch and always the endless charity balls

Their swagger of feminist freedom rode on
Someone else's back. This Maria who has
Left the intimacy of her two daughters home
Scratches the word *Manila, Manila, Manila*

With her thumbnail each time she scrubs
The kitchen stains, her heart in two places.
Sometimes she resists, an *I am!* here or
Forgot the coffee sorry there. Away

From these tedious pranks the Mission
Bulges in its Pentecostal fife and glue—
The choice is this, or that darker side
In the shadow of that Hard Rock Café

An Australian hand job for fifty. On
Sundays and any of the 27 public holidays
They gather in Central, the world's most
Expensive sidewalk of banks, boutiques

5-star hotels. To remove their nuisance
An editorial suggested opening up
Underground car parks for this potluck
For this Maria, out-of-sight, in the violence

Of disappearance fucked as woman, fucked
As worker, fucked as Filipina, color them
The same. One can tell in their voices
That group from Luneta, those from Quiapo

That one by the fountain, they're from
Divisoria, all here: a dollar will win
At Lucky 9 over a plate of *adobo*, listening
To someone else's letter from home

I'll make it here and send it home money
Order, clowning for the photograph machine
Some guitar and song. But Maria is saying
Puta this, *Puta* that, *Puta* them

On this Sunday Star Ferry crossing
To Central, *Puta! Puta! Puta!* That was not
Her birth certificate but has become her
Passport now, ripping up the pink Hello

Kitty doll made by her half-sister
In neighboring Shenzhen, piece by piece
To the disdainful expatriate's stare
And tossing them into Queen Victoria harbor

Against the rolling thud of waves
Against this third-class crossing
Whispering *Do not pass this violence on*
Oh no Mary of God down to the last piece.

FANTASY OR SCIENCE FICTION, ANYONE?

It was three years ago, and hey, it was not easy moving through a cluster of tourists milling thick on that weekend in Tsim Sha Tsui's Hong Kong Cultural Centre. Showcase for Hong Kong's arts and culture. With their fanny packs and bottled water, they were picking their way through the CDs and books and posters, but mostly their eyes hung tired from too many buffets and too many trinkets. Locals were there too, looking for their identity they thought was buried in the countless black-and-white photographic books of its recent colonial past.

I made it to a supervisor with a burnished nameplate *Shirley* over the breast pocket of her dark power suit. I told her I was looking for books by Hong Kong writers. She looked at me as if I'd asked for the latest report of alien abduction on Lantau Island.

"No books," she finally blurted out.

I wanted to say there were books there, it was not my imagination. Among the shelves and shelves of fantasy and science fiction, there were Bronte, Lawrence, Maugham, Dickens, Austen, Hardy, Hemingway, James Clavell's *Noble House,* recent reprints of Richard Mason's *World of Suzie*

Wong and Han Suyin's *A Many Splendoured Thing.* Instead I mentioned Xi Xi, P.K. Leung, Xu Xi, Louise Ho, Agnes Lam. "No, no books," Shirley repeated and turned to attend to the cash register.

Wow, amazing! This was *the* Hong Kong Cultural Centre, the taxpayer-supported showcase of the arts and culture, and I could not find a book by a Hong Kong writer, not even by expat or hyphenated writers such as Edmund Blunden or Lu Xun.

I left the HKCC and visited some other bookstores on both sides of the harbor: Swindon, YMCA, and Times Bookshop; Alexandra House's Bookazine, Exchange Square's HK Book Centre and Wellington House's Continental Books; and the outlets at both terminals of the Star Ferry.

Same result. Nothing by HK writers, their shelves bulging with the same titles as those at the HKCC, as if a book distributor had monopolized the market, in the process controlling the literary culture of Hong Kong, promoting a set of anglophile, canonical authors while denying the existence of any other. Hey, marketing used as an instrument for imperialism, so effective that it continued sixteen years after the announcement that Hong Kong was to be returned to China—another example that the victims are better at mimicking and reproducing the colonial values.

Two days later the publisher of my new novel *Chinese Opera* talked me into a signing at the Kowloon terminal of the Star Ferry. Sales were brisk, but I was struck by the remarks made by a well-to-do Chinese businessman wearing a fancy Rolex and carrying a Halliburton briefcase, who had picked up a copy of the novel, scanned the blurbs, set it down, and said to me, walking away, "Only the English can write novels."

I was reminded that back home in the United States, a nation-state with a cultural and political history twice as long as Hong Kong's, we were still struggling with the same kind of cultural imperialism. The books found at the Hong Kong Cultural Centre had the exact same titles that spilled from a typical backwater college bookstore outside of New York, Chicago or Los Angeles. Likewise, aside from independent bookstores, it was difficult to find books by non-white authors, with the exception of a few by writers such as Toni Morrison, Amy Tan and Sherman Alexie.

Within the cultural parameters of such an environment, it was no wonder that Hong Kong was immersed in the who-am-I discussion that proposed using *the mother tongue* as the language of instruction in the public schools. The president of Baptist University believed it should be *Cantonese*, and went on television to say it, but some others were not so sure that it should not be *Mandarin*.

Just before I left town, I was tempted to interview Martin Lee to see if his Mandarin had improved since he used it as his native font in Beijing in 1985 when he represented the Hong Kong interests in the handover negotiations, but decided that the better answer can be found in Jackie Chan's movie *Who Am I* in this post-colonial period of indefinite hyphens and blurring boundaries.

LOOKING FOR A GAME

Another year out of the country, and my first stop is Hong Kong, arriving shortly after its much-heralded return to China after close to 200 years of British colonial rule. A quick look in the thick metropolitan telephone directory for close to seven million persons found the Hong Kong Contract Bridge Association. Later I find out that under a special agreement, Hong Kong is a separate entity in the World Bridge Federation, as in the Olympics, and is grouped in Zone 6 that includes China and Taiwan, as well as Japan, Indonesia, Thailand, Singapore, Philippines, India, Pakistan, Malaysia, and Macau, a tiny Portuguese colony of seven square miles with half a million people just fifty-five jetboat minutes west of Hong Kong that will also be returned to China in less than two years.

Within three days and one phone call leading indefinitely to another, I looked for a game and a partner. The bridge scene in Hong Kong is exceptionally hierarchical, perhaps a throwback to the colonial exercise of power and class: most of the weekly four or five games are tournament rated, several awarding gold points, Hong Kong CBA gold points. Most of the games are team events that are year long, ongoing venues that do not admit interim new entries. Partnerships are well established, in this club that has more than five hundred members, I was assured.

Over my many phone calls, several players mentioned that Jackie was always looking for a partner. In the U.S. clubs that I've played in, there has always been that last player to find a partner, always standing at the door, the last king in the neighborhood to be included in anything at all, the one assigned to play right field and bat last. So I waited on calling him up for a game until I was absolutely sure that there was no other option.

Yes, Jackie was available for the next two-session event, for gold points, at the club located next to the old juvenile prison, police station and post office. It seemed that everything in Hong Kong is located next to a former police station or former post office. It takes 500 points, including 50 gold, to make Life Master in the HKCBA, so I had anticipated a large turnout. So we waited, Jackie and I filling out an American Contract Bridge League-cloned convention card before the 2 p.m. Saturday starting time. We played 2/1 game force with so many toys including a strange Flannery variation and a combination of Neapolitan 2 ♦ and multi-color 2 ♦ that would have given Kay Fergie, my favorite Spokane partner, a headache.

A two-session gold point event at a club with more than 500 members turned out to be a 5½-table game with 22 boards each session. What happened to the other members? Had they been exiled to the prison or the police station, or express-mailed out of the country by their partners for agreement violations or psychs?

The average age of the other 21 players was about the same as ACBL's—in the late 50s. Likewise, there was a high percentage with college degrees. The numbers also indicate that there are close to ten times more duplicate players per capita in the U.S. than in Hong Kong. But unlike ACBL's division of 65 women to 35 men, there was only one woman player that Saturday, Ella Graca, who had represented Hong Kong in international play and who came in one place ahead of Jackie and me.

The club roster reflected a 5-to-1 male-to-female ratio, a number that I anticipate will increase dramatically for men when I play in China in the months ahead. If the players in this event are any indication, there are fewer smoking bridge players in Hong Kong than in the U.S., a phenomenon that will certainly change under Chinese rule.

So I'm playing with Jackie who is a HKCBA Life Master. First place in the event will earn more than eight gold points. Yes, eight, that is not a typo. The first hand is picked up, and in the middle of our auction, Jackie answers his cell phone. What do you do when your partner across the table whips out his cellular and yells into it while bidding 2 ♠ between two passes? Better yet, what do I make of all the Rolex watches, very exclusive golf clubs, yacht clubs, jockey clubs, private dinner clubs, the US$400 for an all-day haircut-and-massage, and the more than 200 Ferraris in a city that can claim no more than maybe fifty miles of crowded highways? It seems that the people of Hong Kong have rendered their lives into icons and symbols, as if to prove to themselves that they, under the continuing legacy of British colonial rule, are not immigrants in their own city. And they are doing this with a vengeance. In fact, excess wealth has bought one Hong Kong bridge player his personal, annual Shanghai-Hong Kong match, with a place reserved for him on the team.

Hong Kong residents have become the consummate consumers in their version of late capitalism, and the cell phone has been adopted as the ultimate accessory of Hong Kong's middle class though it does not work in the much-traveled underground transportation system. So Jackie answers his cell phone nine times in the first five rounds, finally explaining that his father is old-fashioned and refuses to believe that his phone's dial is set wrong and won't let his son change it.

I recall that in a 1981 article in *The Bridge World*, Ron Klinger was not particularly kind in his assessment of the quality of bridge in Hong Kong. What he failed to mention was the speed of the play. It's slowness drove me crazy: in the auction, on the opening lead, on each card played in defense, in declarer play, when nearly every deal could have been thrown against the wall for the same result. What can they be possibly thinking about? Perhaps this leisurely pace mimics the colonial class structure in which the ruling British played their bridge sipping gin and tonics and smoking 555s in isolated, social club settings, removed and distanced from the motions of everyday life.

Every card was played as if in preparation for a progressive squeeze or to escape an impending trump coup. If the unnecessary slowness is an accurate indication of the quality of their bridge logic, then I count myself blessed in not knowing enough Cantonese to understand their extensive postmortems of each deal, which also contribute to the slow tempo. The two-board eleven-round session took four hours and six minutes, an average of twenty-two minutes per round. It did occur to me that this pace may be compensation for the rat race Hong Kong residents experience in the rest of their entrepreneurial lives.

Immediately outside the club and throughout the rest of Hong Kong, cars, trucks and even buses are driven dangerously above the speed limit. Many schools are in session six days a week. People shop and work until well past midnight seven days a week. Here at the bridge table, Jackie as declarer closes his eyes and rests while his opponents decide which one of 13 cards to play, and—much, much later—which one of two cards to play.

For all of that, Jackie is okay, and his bridge is quite sound, as one can see from the following two hands and auction. We reached a good diamond slam on 27 high-card points.

Jackie	Me
♠ KQ6	♠ A743
♥ KQ92	♥ AJT
♦ AK76	♦ J9832
♣ 83	♣ 7
1 ♦	1 ♠
2 ♥	3 ♦
4 ♠	6 ♦
Pass	

Even though we didn't place, I enjoyed playing with Jackie. It turns out that he's always looking for a partner who can play two deals in less than fifteen minutes. Now, if only the cell phone can be checked at the door.

PARTNERSHIPS

In Hong Kong, I arrived at a tournament team game a polite thirty minutes before the event. It took Shirley and me, a partnership of four games, about thirty seconds to go over our convention card. Leading from fourth best, to third or fifth best, no? Yes.

Looking around the room, I found most of the players busily reviewing their bidding systems and defense carding. Accustomed to a different cultural environment in which a pre-game conversation would more likely focus on the latest Monica Lewinsky gossip or one's children or grand-children, I was surprised most of the dialogue was actually directed on the convention card.

At an adjacent table, an established partnership was testing each other on the system they had used together for more than two decades. One of them pulled out from his briefcase a taped-together piece of paper measuring no less than half the size of the playing table, which unfolded their entire bidding sequences in fine black, green, blue, and red print.

1 ♦ opening in third or fourth seat? Promises 4-4-3-2 or at least 3-4-3-3 or 4-3-3-3 distribution. Shirley and I looked at each other without rolling our eyes. 2 ♦ opening? It can be a

preemptive in spades or hearts, or it could be... I could not bear to hear the rest of this interrogation.

On one level this pre-game review reflected the absence of trust in the partnership, the suspicion that one's partner is going to forget a convention in use for twenty years. On another it suggested that the players had no grasp of the fundamentals of bidding that would rescue them in the event a seldom-used or rogue convention came up. And finally, the endless list of added-on conventions mirrored Hong Kong's preoccupation with food, specifically the buffet: there are literally thousands of buffets everyday, buffet breakfast, buffet lunch, buffet high tea, buffet dinner. A little of this; a little of that. One must have a little of everything, even if it is incompatible with everything else in the system. Perhaps talking about the trendiest buffet is better than talking about Monica Lewinsky or, in the case of Hong Kong, who had just committed suicide because of a stock market catastrophe.

But in this power play, the partner who was the victim of this interrogation looked too much like he had been in prison for too long, that same rueful expression while waiting for his teammates to finish the round at the other table, what Nietzsche had said about Christians, that you can tell from their faces that they don't enjoy what they do.

In the final round of the four, nine-deals match, our squad was playing against the only other undefeated team. My partner and I were North-South, on this deal:

```
Dlr: North        ♠ T65
Vul: Both         ♥ A98643
                  ♦ T
                  ♣ A97

♠ KQJ4                        ♠ A832
♥ K52                         ♥ JT7
♦ J985                        ♦ KQ72
♣ K8                          ♣ QT

                  ♠ 97
                  ♥ Q
                  ♦ A543
                  ♣ J65432
```

West	North	East	South
	Shirley		*Me*

East led the ♦ K, taken in dummy. Shirley then played the ♥ Q, ducked all around. Yes, it was an error for West not to cover, but suppose North had ♥ AJT — then it would be a mistake to cover. Anyway, Shirley ruffed a diamond to hand and played the ♥ A , followed by a low heart.

Shirley ruffed again when West continued diamonds, then she followed with the ♣ A and another club. The 2-2 club split let her get home with eight tricks for plus 110.

Our teammates had finished their round first. They were standing by the doorway, looking sullen, one of them as if he had just done something very wrong, and the other as if he had just retired from a lifetime of teaching second graders. It turned out that on the same deal, North passed, giving our teammates the opportunity—which they seized—to reach their spade game, played by East.

South led the ♥ Q and the resulting crossruff was brutal. North and South made each of their trumps separately and they also took tricks with their three aces. Down five for minus 500. The net loss was 390, or 9 IMPs. Our team lost by 8 IMPs.

As we walked to the elevator, surely we must have looked like four gray persons just waiting for someone to take us home and make us hot chocolate.

A LETTER HOME

I've encountered some problems in trying to find knowledgeable literary types to serve on the panel you've consented to chair in the upcoming literary festival, "Literary Contexts: Publishing, Editing, Translation."

By far the biggest bookstore in Hong Kong is Swindon, Times and Caves a distant second. It also owns the books-and-CDs concession in the gross, huge, public-funded, pink-tiled, architectural monstrosity Hong Kong Cultural Centre [sic] located in Tsim Sha Tsui, Kowloon's tourist center at the beginning of the Golden Mile. This arts center books the largest events, and is always packed when Anne-Sophie Mutter or Isaac Stern or the Bolshoi comes to town, but half empty when the Beijing opera presents. It carries about ten feet of fiction in English, and a person can get anything by Lawrence, Hemingway, Conrad or Margaret Drabble. But try to find a book by a Hong Kong writer, you might as well step out of the building and dive into Victoria Harbour.

I asked Annabella Li, the managing director of Swindon, if she would serve on your panel, and she said no, no, no. The same thing with the book and cultural editors of the largest circulating English-language newspaper, the *South China Morning Post*. It reviews some ten to twenty books a week, almost all of them set in western culture. Both the book editor Elisabeth Tacey and cultural editor Kevin Kwong (I think I've been here too long—being able to bring up their names from memory when I can't even remember my street number back home in Idaho) also said no, because of editorial conflict since they'll be covering the festival. The director of the Arts Development Council (same as our National Endowment for the Arts—in fact it uses NEA-cloned application forms) that turned down my funding proposal three times, Terence Chang, also declined but mentioned that he will be in the audience, as well as three ADC members.

I continue to be astounded by all the secrets in Hong Kong. Hong Kong author Xu Xi's novel *Hong Kong Rose* talks about the constructed histories. Maxine Hong Kingston says "they must try to confuse their offspring as well, who, I suppose, threaten them in similar ways—always trying to get things straight, always trying to name the unspeakable." During the Q/A following Xu Xi's reading two nights ago, a friend asked the unspeakable, if she would expand on the social norms and lies in Hong Kong.

My friend got severe shocked looks from several Hong Kongers in the audience sitting next to her, looks that said first a foreigner has recognized the secret, and next, that she would dare to bring it up in public. In my literature class yesterday afternoon, after considerable pushing, my students finally started talking about Xu Xi's novel. They did not like my requiring a novel written by a contemporary Hong Kong author in an English class, and they most certainly did not want to talk about the secrets in their parents' lives. Maybe in order to survive from displacement, dislocation, and other forms of exile, the emigrants—and here I believe that almost everyone in Hong Kong was an emigrant at one time or another, the Tankas being the only exception—must construct these histories that totally frustrate their children. Joan Didion has said that the future always looks golden when the past is forgotten, at least in the California context.

The case of Paul Theroux's *Kowloon Tong* prompts a re-examination of the presentation of Hong Kong from a foreign novelist's point of view, such as Richard Mason's *The World of Suzie Wong* and Han Suyin's *Love is a Many Splendored Thing*. In the first week I was here at a small Tsim Sha Tsui shop, a clerk was chasing out a couple of British kids in school uniform, yelling in Cantonese, "Out, out, get out, British boys." A naïve observer might conclude that she was racist (which she might well be, for good reason), or another person would interpret her words as warning off British school children who shoplift with institutionalized immunity.

In the year 1800, before British occupation, there were some 500 to 2,000 residents in Hong Kong, depending on who was counting whom. But in some 175 years of British rule, wave after wave of emigrants came to Hong Kong until its present seven million inhabitants, of which about five thousand are Americans. Local and regional culture and identity had never been an issue, the Brits saw to that. But since 1982-4 when Margaret Thatcher signed the handover documents in Beijing, the fastest growing industry here in Hong Kong focuses on attempts to answer the political identity question of "Who am I?" and I for one think that Jackie Chan did a better job. The publicly-funded HK$580 million museum of history is under construction, and the big issue here is how to represent the June 4, 1989 Tiananmen Square incident, even when Tiananmen Square is in Beijing, one thousand two hundred and twenty two miles away. The answers have ranged from getting a tank (purchased from the Chinese arms manufacturer Norinco?) for display, to fresh floral garlands for China's People's Liberation Army, while committees of cultural personalities have debated whether the concept of *hybrid* or *fusion* is a more accurate description of Hong Kong.

It might be safer in Faulkner's Yoknapatawpha County, Mississippi.

BITTER MELONS

Sixty years ago this was my universe where I lived and played. Now I was back as an impatient and sweaty tourist from another post-colonial country some six thousand miles away bursting in air, as if I were late for a meeting, a bumpy voice recorder hitched to my waist. Despite the massive land use alterations resulting from the political reclamation and entrepreneurial ventures, actually I knew exactly where I was, headed home via a series of diagonal crossings and trespassing shortcuts. Or more correctly, where home was, in the last apartment building on that hill, there on a short street ending at the backside of the Royal Observatory where its seasonal typhoon signals were visible to every mariner in the harbor of this crown colony under King George VI, Number Ten being the severest.

Most of the buildings had disappeared, and the vegetation as well, including the expansive banyan trees, now replaced by an occasional *bauhinia* bush planted to reverse the racial and political hegemony. Though I may not have known exactly who I was at that jostled moment, I knew precisely where I was in time, and I was in a hurry. Here, the Chanticleer bakery with its fresh, creamy napoleons across the street from the resident

Argyll and most-feared Gurkha barracks, next the comics book stand, both temptations on the walk home from the Canadian Immaculate Conception elementary school where I learned to tuck slide into second base, demonstrated one recess by an eager nun in flowing white habit.

Here the trek was interrupted by a residential development of infinite small houses, each with its narrow stone steps leading to doors of equally colorless homes, except for their sky-blue trim. Several men suddenly appeared, including one who looked Indian or Pakistani, even though his skin was too light. They wanted to know what I was looking for, *Torpedo Alley*, they called their neighborhood in Chinese without smiling. But I knew better, they were fooling me, looking at the harbor some two hundred feet in elevation below us. It was clear they did not want me there, now as well as sixty years ago. So I explained that as a writer I was not balanced, I had just lost my way to the ferry terminal. The Indian or Pakistani man said he understood, since his wife was also a writer, of novels, he said, his eyes still a patch of doubt, and pointed, downhill first, then to the right.

Clutching my recorder then, I went downhill first, but once out of their sight around the next corner, I turned onto a muddy field where several pages were missing. Gone were the small houses and concrete sidewalk. Instead, sparse vegetable plots garnished the landscape from edge to edge. Two men in their thirties came up from one of them, though I knew they were really in their eighties, because as witness I could identify them, coming around every afternoon collecting metal, glass or paper they'd sell for recycling, rain or shine.

One of them pointed down to a row of garlic stems by his feet and said it was his. He directed his finger to the next row and said these fat cabbages were his friend's. Then he said the last row of tiny, dark green bitter melons belonged to both of them, tended most carefully, even in the wet and windy summer typhoon season, to keep them from rotting, he added at the end as I continued downhill to the ferry terminal.

By this time the men from Torpedo Alley had caught up with me and my transformational tricks in hallucination or dream. Like their security predecessors, they scolded me and escorted me to the gate, just when I was perfectly balanced on a high banyan limb. I used to live near here, some sixty years ago, I was sure of it.

Look here, at the Star Ferry terminal then, I skip the *Morning Star* and the *Meridian Star* and wait for the *Celestial Star* for the crossing. In my hands the recorder clutches the words most dear to those missing pages for which I live on my way home.

About the Author

In the last fifty years, Alex Kuo has taught writing, literature and cultural studies at several universities in the United States, China and Hong Kong.

His work has received three National Endowment for the Arts awards and grants from the United Nations and the States of Idaho and Washington. Among his eleven books, *Lipstick and Other Stories* won the American Book Award.

He has held a Senior Fulbright to China and a Lingnan professorship to Hong Kong. In 2008 Fudan University invited him to be its first Distinguished Writer-in-Residence. Currently he holds an adjunct professorship at Beijing Forestry University.

www.alexkuo.org

EXPLORE ASIA WITH BLACKSMITH BOOKS

From retailers around the world or from *www.blacksmithbooks.com*

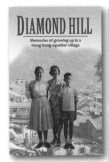

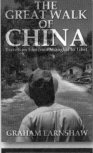

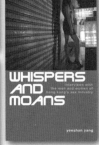